D0348351

First Names

Collins
London and Glasgow

General Editor
W. T. McLeod

First Published 1967
Latest Reprint 1983

ISBN 0 00 458748 0

© **William Collins Sons & Co. Ltd., 1967**

Printed in Great Britain by
Collins Clear-Type Press

FOREWORD

Interest in names is peculiarly widespread. They are a by-product of human activity as important to the hopeful parent and the inquiring child as to the philologist or historian. In the scope of this small work we have tried to include those names which have been prominent in the modern cultural development of Britain. We have made no attempt to capture all the individual variations and inventions that have occurred, especially in recent years, as these are far too numerous and, except in rare cases, do not have a wide application. We provide a guide to the pronunciation of the names, and describe briefly the history and development of each one. Etymologies have been kept simple; we use 'Old German' to describe both Old High and Middle High German and we use 'Welsh' and 'Irish', so that 'Gaelic' refers exclusively to Scottish Gaelic. Occasionaly the term 'Celtic' indicates a lack of evidence about which branch of that language a name first developed in. The short sketches on each main entry show how names were affected by social and political events, by literature, and by the influence of outstanding personalities, and how, in their turn, they reflect the beliefs and aspirations of English speaking peoples.

The book was compiled in our reference department by Sandra Bance, B.A. Hons., Mary Laird and Charles Wacher, under the supervision of Mr. A. G. Hepburn, A.L.A., Head Librarian of the Mitchell Library, Glasgow, and Mr. R. E. Adams, B.A., A.L.A., of the National Library of Scotland, Edinburgh.

PRONUNCIATION

ā	as in	mate	a	as in	pat
ē	,,	mete	e	,,	pet
ī	,,	mite	i	,,	pit
ō	,,	mote	o	,,	pot
ū	,,	mute	u	,,	nut

à	as in	father	th	as in	thin
e̱	,,	her	TH	,,	thine
ȯȯ	,,	boot	zh	,,	leisure
oo	,,	foot	ch	,,	church
ow	,,	owl	H	,,	loch

The symbol ′ follows stressed syllables

A

AARON *m.* (*e'ręn*)

possibly from the Hebrew for 'mountaineer', or an Egyptian name of
obscure meaning. It is connected with
the Arabic names Harun and Haroun.
In the Old Testament Aaron was the
brother of Moses and first High Priest
of Israel. The name has been in use
since the Reformation, but has never
been common.

ABBEY, ABBIE *see* **ABIGAIL**

ABE, ABIE *see* **ABEL, ABRAHAM**

ABEL *m.* (*ā'bęl*)

from Hebrew, the word may be connected with that for 'breath' or for
'son'. In the Old Testament Abel was
the second son of Adam and Eve. The
name has been in use in England since
before the Norman Conquest, and is
still found occasionally. The short forms
include Abe, Abie and Nab.

ABELARD *m.* (*ab'ĕlàd*)

This is a medieval French name derived from the Old German meaning 'noble and resolute'. It is best known from the 12th century French philosopher, Pierre Abelard (*see* ADALARD).

ABIGAIL *f.* (*ab'igāl*)

from the Hebrew meaning 'father rejoiced'. It was the name of one of King David's wives and was much used in England during the 16th and 17th centuries, when many Old Testament names were popular. It degenerated into a term for a lady's maid and declined, but it is now being revived. The short forms include Abbie, Abbey and Gail (q.v.).

ABNER *m.* (*ab'nĕ*)

from the Hebrew words for 'father' and 'light'. It was the name of Saul's cousin, who was also commander of Saul's army. In England, it came into use after the Reformation, and it is still found occasionally in North America.

ABRAHAM *m.* (*āb'reham*)

This is the name of the Old Testament patriarch, which was changed from the form Abram, 'high father', to Abraham, 'father of many'. It was used in England regularly after the Reformation and became popular in North America. There the abbreviation Abe, as for the name of the President Abe Lincoln, was widely used. Other short forms are Abie, Ham and Bram. Bram is sometimes used as a name in its own right.

ABRAM *see* **ABRAHAM**

ABSALOM *m.* (*ab'selem*)

from the Hebrew words meaning 'father' and 'peace'. In the Old Testament Absalom was the son of King David and Michal. The name was popular in England in the 12th and 13th centuries when the French spelling, Absolon, was often used. It is very rarely found today.

ABSOLON *see* **ABSALOM**

ADA *f.* (ā′dę)

Sometimes used as a pet form for Adelaide and Adeline (qq.v.), this is also a name in its own right, possibly derived from the Old German Eda or Etta meaning 'happy'. It was fashionable in Britain in the late 18th and 19th centuries.

ADAH *f.* (ā′dę)

This name is often confused with Ada but is in fact derived from the Hebrew word for 'ornament'. It occurs in the Old Testament book of Genesis and is one of the oldest names still in use. It was popular in England in the 19th century and is still used occasionally in North America.

ADAIR *m.* (ęder′)

This is an old Scottish name derived from the Gaelic meaning 'of the oak-tree ford'. It is still in use, both as a Christian name and surname, but is not common.

ADALARD *m.* (*ad'ęlàd*)

from Old German Adalhard, meaning 'noble and resolute'. There was an 8th century saint of this name, who founded an abbey in Saxony. It has been very rarely used in this country.

ADALFUNS *see* **ALPHONSUS**

ADAM *m.* (*ad'ęm*)

from the Hebrew meaning 'red', possibly referring either to the skin colour, or to the earth from which God formed the first man, in the Old Testament. The name was not used by the Jews, but was adopted by the Irish as early as the 7th century, when St. Adamnan, 'Adam the Little', was Abbot of Iona. It was very common in the 13th century, and has been used ever since, particularly in Scotland. Adamina is a rare feminine form.

ADAMINA *see* **ADAM**

ADAMNAN *see* **ADAM**

ADELA *f.* (*adāl'ę*)

from the Old German meaning 'noble'. It was common among the Normans, who brought it to England. One of William the Conqueror's daughters had this name. It died out but later became fashionable among the Victorians, sometimes in the French form Adèle which is still regularly used.

ADELAIDE *f.* (*ad'ęlād*)

derived from Old German words meaning 'noble and kind'. It was common for centuries on the Continent but came to Britain in 1830 when Adelaide of Saxe-Coburg became Queen. Adelaide, capital city of S. Australia, was named after this popular Queen. Ada (q.v.) is sometimes used as a pet form.

ADÈLE *see* **ADELA**

ADELICE, ADELISE *see* **ALICE**

ADELINE *f.* (*ad'ęlēn, ad'ęlīn*)

Like Adelaide this name is derived from the Old German for 'noble'. It was first

cited in England in Domesday Book, and
was common during the Middle Ages.
After that it disappeared until the
Victorian Gothic revival. Recently it
has had another revival.

ADOLPHA *see* ADOLPHUS

ADOLPHUS *m.* (*adol'fĕs*)

from the Old German Athalwolf meaning 'noble wolf'. Adolphus is a latinised
form of the German name which came
to Britain as a result of the Hanoverian
Succession. It was used occasionally
in the 18th and 19th centuries, but is
now rarely found. Adolpha is an equally
rare feminine form.

ADRIAN *m.* (*ā'driĕn*)

from the Latin meaning 'man from
Adria', and the name of the Roman
Emperor Hadrianus, who built the wall
across Northern England. It has been
used from Roman times; a St. Adrian
was martyred in the 4th century and
another helped organise the English
Church in the 7th century. It was com-

mon from the 12th century, perhaps on account of the English Pope Adrian IV, and has become popular again recently. Adriana is a rare feminine form, the French Adrienne being more popular today. Adrianne is also found.

ADRIANA, ADRIANNE, ADRIENNE
see ADRIAN

AEGIDIUS see GILES

AEMILIANUS see EMLYN

AEMILIUS see EMILY

AENEAS m. (ēnē′ęs)

the name of the legendary hero of Virgil's *Aeneid*, who is said to have escaped from the Sack of Troy to Italy, and laid the first foundations of the civilisation of Rome. The name has been given in Britain since the Renaissance but has never been common, although in Scotland it has been used to transliterate the Gaelic Aonghus (*see* ANGUS).

AETHELMAER see AYLMER

AGACE, AGACIA *see* AGATHA

AGATHA *f.* (ag′ęthę)

from the Greek meaning 'good woman', the name of a 3rd century martyr and saint. The name was popular during the Middle Ages in various forms, including the French Agace and the Latin Agacia, but it is now rather rare. The short form is Aggie.

AGGIE *see* AGATHA

AGNES *f.* (ag′nis)

from the Greek word meaning 'pure'. There was an early Christian martyr called Agnes, and the name was very popular from the 12th to 16th centuries in England. It had many forms, including Annis, Annice, Annes and Agneta. Inez is the anglicised form of the Spanish Inés. Agnes has always been popular in Scotland with its diminutives Nessie and Nessa. In Wales it becomes Nest and Nesta.

AGNETA *see* AGNES

AIDAN *m.* (*ā'dẹn*)

from the diminutive form of the Irish word for 'fire'. It was the name of a 7th century Irish monk of Lindisfarne in Northumbria and enjoyed a brief revival during the 19th century. It is still used occasionally.

AILEEN *f.* (*ā'lēn*)

from the Irish form of Helen (q.v.). It is popular in the British Isles today, especially in Scotland and Ireland.

AILEMAR *see* AYLMER

AIMÉ *see* ESMÉ

AIMÉE *see* AMY

AINE *see* AITHNE

AIR *see* ERIC

AITHNE *f.* (*eth'ni*)

from the Irish meaning 'little fire', it has been popular for centuries in Ireland. In legend Aine is queen of the fairies in South Munster. As a result of the revival of Celtic names it is coming back into use in Scotland and Ireland. Modern variants include Ethne and Eithne.

ALAIN, ALEIN, *see* ALAN

ALAN *m.* (*al'ęn*)

probably from the Irish meaning 'harmony'. It has appeared in various forms from early times. In England it first became popular after the Norman Conquest as Alain and Alein, the French forms. These developed into Alleyne which is preserved as a surname. Alan, Allan and Allen are in use today. Alanna is a rare feminine form.

ALASDAIR, ALASTAIR, ALISTAIR, ALISTER *see* ALEXANDER

ALBAN *m.* (*awl'bęn*)

from the Latin Albanus, meaning 'man from Alba', and the name of the first British martyr. Various legends give the town of St. Albans as the birthplace and the place of execution of this saint. The name was never common, but it was revived under the influence of the Oxford Movement in the 19th century. Albin and Albinus are variants which appear occasionally.

ALBERIC, ALBERY see AUBREY

ALBERT *m.* (*al'bęt*)

from the Old German words meaning 'noble' and 'bright'. The Old English form was Ethelbert, famous for the Kentish king who welcomed St. Augustine. This was replaced after the conquest by the French Aubert. Halbert was a Northern English variant. Albert became very popular after the marriage of Queen Victoria to Prince Albert of Saxe-Coburg. The feminine forms Alberta and Albertine are rare. Bert and Bertie are short forms.

ALBERTA, ALBERTINE see ALBERT

ALBIN, ALBINUS see ALBAN

ALBINA *f.* (*albē'nę*)

from the Latin meaning 'white'. The name was often used in the 17th and

18th centuries, but is rarely found today. The Italian form Albinia was introduced into England by the Cecil family and has been used by them since.

ALBINIA *see* ALBINA

ALDO *see* ALDOUS

ALDOUS m. *(awl´dus)*

from the Old German Aldo, meaning 'old'. It has been used in the eastern counties of England since the 13th century and has given rise to various surnames like Aldhouse and Aldiss. Aldo is still in use in North America. The writer Aldous Huxley is a famous modern British example.

ALESSANDRA *see* SANDRA

ALETHEA f. *(alē´thēē)*

from the Greek word meaning 'truth'. It was much used in the 17th century in England. Variant forms include Alethia and Aletia, but only Alethea is now in use.

ALETIA *see* ALETHEA

ALEXANDER *m.* (*alekzán'dẹ*)

from the Greek word meaning 'defender of men'. It was very popular in England in the Middle Ages, appearing often in the French form Alysaundre. In Scotland it has been widely used both in the English form and the Gaelic variants Alasdair, Alastair, Alistair and Alister, with the pronunciation (*a'listẹr*). Sandy is a common pet form. Short forms are Alex, Alec and Lex.

ALEXANDRA *f.* (*alekzàn'drẹ*)

feminine form of Alexander (q.v.). It was in use in England by the 13th century, but only became popular with the marriage of the Prince of Wales (later King Edward VII) to Princess Alexandra of Denmark. Sandra (q.v.) was originally the Italian diminutive form, but has become established as a name in its own right.

ALEXIS *m. and f.* (*alek'sis*)

from the Greek, meaning 'helper' or 'defender'. The name is common in

Russia and has been used occasionally in the 20th century in Britain and North America for both boys and girls.

ALF, ALFIE see **ALFRED**

ALFONSO see **ALPHONSUS**

ALFRED m. (al'fred)

from two Old English words meaning 'elf' (hence 'good') and 'counsel'. It is also a possible development of the name Ealdfrith, meaning 'old peace', and was the name of a 7th century king of Northumbria, sometimes being written Alfrid. When its spelling was latinised, the name developed into Alured and then into Avery, which survives as a surname. The original Alfred was reintroduced in the 18th century and became very popular in the 19th. Alf, Alfie and Fred are diminutives and there is a rare feminine form Alfreda.

ALFREDA see **ALFRED**

ALFRID see **ALFRED**

ALGERNON *m.* (*al'jenon*)

from the Norman French nickname meaning 'with whiskers'. It was uncommon from Tudor times up to the 19th century, when its use became general. The usual diminutives are Algie or Algy.

ALGIE, ALGY *see* ALGERNON

ALIA *see* ELLA

ALICE *f.* (*al'is*)

from the Old German word for 'nobility'. It originally had the form Adelice or Adelise. A number of variants remained popular from the Middle Ages until the 17th century, when it declined in favour. It was revived again in the 19th century together with the variant Alicia, and achieved immortality in Lewis Carroll's *Alice in Wonderland*. Alison (q.v.) is a variant which became popularly established at the same time as Alice, especially in Scotland. Alys is the Welsh form.

ALICIA *see* **ALICE**

ALINE *f.* (*ă'lēn, a'lēn*)

originally a short form of Adeline (q.v.) but now definitely established, as an independent name, much more popular than the declining Adeline. Variant forms are Arleen and Arline.

ALISON *f.* (*al'isẹn*)

originally a diminutive of Alice (q.v.) adopted in the 13th century, but soon treated as a separate name. It has remained popular since, especially in Scotland. Pet forms include Ally, Ailie and Elsie.

ALLAN, ALLEN, ALLEYNE *see* **ALAN**

ALLOYS *see* **ALOYSIUS**

ALLY, AILIE *see* **ALISON**

ALMA *f.* (*al'mẹ*)

There are many opinions about the derivation of this name. It possibly had its origin in the Hebrew word for 'maiden', the Latin for 'kind' or the

Italian for 'soul'. The name became very popular after the battle of Alma in the Crimean War, and it is still found occasionally.

ALOYSIUS *m. (alōish'ęs)*

This is a latinisation of Aloys, an old Provençal form of Louis (q.v.). There was a popular Spanish saint of this name in the 16th century and Roman Catholics continue to use the name in this country.

ALPHONSUS *m. (alfon'sęs)*

from Old German Adalfuns meaning 'noble ready', Alphonsus being the latinised form. The name is most common in Spain as Alfonso. It is only rarely found in Britain.

ALTHEA *f. (al'thēę)*

from the Greek for 'wholesome'. It appears to have been introduced to England with various other classical names during the Stuart period, and appeared in the charming lyric by

Lovelace *To Althea from Prison*. It is still found, though not very widely.

ALURED *see* ALFRED

ALVIN *m. (al'vin)*

from the Old German meaning either 'friend of all' or 'noble friend'. This is a very rare name in Britain today, but is still found fairly frequently in North America.

ALYS *see* ALICE

ALYSAUNDRE *see* ALEXANDER

AMABEL *f. (am'ebel)*

from the Latin for 'lovable'. It has been in use in England in various forms since the 12th century. The short form Mabel (q.v.) early became established as an independent name. There was a revival of the use of Amabel in the 19th century.

AMANDA *f. (eman'de)*

from the Latin meaning 'lovable'. It appears first in Restoration plays, where many names from classical sources were introduced or fabricated. It has remained in use since and is still popular. Mandy is a pet form.

AMARYLLIS *f.* (*amҫril'is*)

originally from Greek, probably meaning 'fresh stream', and used by Greek poets as a name for pastoral heroines. It served the same purpose for Latin poets, and was introduced into English poetry in the 17th century. It has been given occasionally.

AMATA *see* AMY

AMBROSE *m.* (*am'brōz*)

from the Greek for 'divine'. There was a 4th century St. Ambrose who was Bishop of Milan, and exerted a strong influence in the West Country. The name is found in Domesday Book and has been used occasionally since. The Welsh name Emrys (q.v.) is derived from Ambrosius Aurelianus the 5th century leader of the Celts against the Saxons. There is a rare feminine form Ambrosine.

AMBROSINE, AMBROSIUS
see **AMBROSE**

AMELIA *f.* (ęmē'lię)

from an Old German word possibly meaning 'labour', and the root of many German names. Another influence on the name's development is the Roman family name, Aemilianus. It was introduced into Britain under the Hanoverian royal line, and was often anglicised to Emily, as in the case of George III's youngest daughter, Princes Emily. The short form is usually Milly.

AMOS *m.* (ā'mos)

from the Hebrew for 'strong'. It was the name of an Old Testament prophet and was adopted by the Puritans after the Reformation in England, when saints' names were in disfavour. Since then it has become common in North America.

AMY *f.* (ā'mi)

from the French meaning 'beloved woman'. There was a 13th century

saint with the Latin form of the name,
Amata, who made it fairly popular,
especially among Roman Catholics.
In the 19th century, Sir Walter Scott's
novel *Kenilworth*, about Amy Robsart,
the tragic wife of the Earl of Leicester,
made the name fashionable, and it is
well known in Britain today. A famous
20th century holder of the name was
Amy Johnson, the pioneer flyer. Aimée,
the French original of this name, has
been used in Britain (*see* ESMÉ).

AMYAS *m.* (*ā'mēes*)

The origin of this name is uncertain but
it is probably derived from the Latin
verb *amare*, meaning 'to love', and can
therefore be regarded as the masculine
form of Amy (q.v.). The modern use
of the name is probably due to Charles
Kingsley's novel *Westward Ho*! in which
the hero is an Elizabethan named Amyas
Leigh.

ANASTASIA *f.* (*anęstá'zię, anęstāz'ię*)

from the Greek meaning 'resurrection',

and the name of a 4th century saint and martyr. It became fashionable in England in the 13th century, though it was usually abbreviated to Anstey or Anstice, which survive today as surnames. It has always been very popular in Russia, and a daughter of the last Czar of Russia, called Anastasia, is said to have escaped from the execution in which the rest of her family died, in 1918. Several books, plays and films have been written about her, and they have made the name better known in Britain in the 20th century. Stacey is a North American pet form.

ANDREA *see* ANDREW

ANDREW *m.* (*an'drŏŏ*)

from the Greek for 'manly', It is the name of the Apostle who is patron saint of Scotland and Russia, and first appears in England in Domesday Book. It has been used in Britain continuously, and has enjoyed particular favour in Scotland. It was chosen by Queen Elizabeth II for her second son, in 1960, and it is one of the commonest boys' names in Britain today. The diminutives include Andy, Dandy (Scots) and Drew. The Italian form, Andrea, is used as a girl's name.

ANDY *see* **ANDREW**

ANEIRIN *see* **ANEURIN**

ANEURIN *m.* (*ǫnoi'rin*)

possibly the Welsh form of Latin Honorius, meaning 'honourable', or a compound of the Welsh words for 'all' and 'gold', with a diminutive ending. It also appears in the form Aneirin. It has always been popular in Wales, with its diminutive Nye, which became familiar as the name of the Labour politician Aneurin Bevan.

ANGEL *see* **ANGELA**

ANGELA *f.* (*an'jęlę*)

from the Latin for 'angel', originally derived from the Greek word meaning 'messenger'. In England it was used regularly as a girl's name, side by side with the masculine form Angel, until it was barred as impious by the Puritans. Angelica enjoyed favour in literary contexts between the 15th and 18th centuries. Angela was revived in the 19th century together with the short-lived Angeline and Angelina.

ANGELICA *see* ANGELA

ANGELINA, ANGELINE *see* ANGELA

ANGUS *m.* (an′gəs)

from the Gaelic Aonghus meaning 'one choice'. It appears in Irish legend and early Celtic church history, and became firmly established in Scotland. The name became associated with the classical myth of Aeneas (q.v.) in the 15th century, and this form was also used.

ANITA *see* ANN

ANN *f.* (an)

from the Hebrew Hannah, meaning 'grace'. Hannah, the name of the mother of the prophet Samuel in the Old Testament, has been in use in

England since the Reformation, and was very popular in North America. The French form Anne was introduced into Britain in the 13th century and the name has enjoyed great popularity since, being the name of six queens and now of the only daughter of Queen Elizabeth II. Diminutives include Nan, Nanny, Nancy (q.v.) and Annie, as well as the variants Anita, Annette and Anona. Ann has often formed part of compounds such as Mary Ann (which became Marian (q.v.) or Marianne), Carol Anne, Joy Anne, etc. Another form, Anna, is very often used.

ANNA *see* ANN, HANNAH

ANNABEL *f.* (*an'ębel*)

possibly from the Latin meaning 'lovable', as a variant of Amabel (q.v.). It's use in Scotland is recorded before that of Ann, though it is now sometimes thought of as a compound of Anna and the Latin *bella*, meaning 'beautiful'. Diminutives include Bel, Belle and Bella.

ANNE, ANNETTE, ANNIE *see* **ANN**

ANNES *see* **AGNES**

ANNIS, ANNICE *see* **AGNES**

ANNORA *see* **HONOR**

ANONA *see* **ANN**

ANTHEA *f.* (*an'thie*)

from the Greek meaning 'flowery'. This name seems to have been introduced by the pastoral poets of the 17th century and it has been in use ever since, although not until the 20th century was it very widely known.

ANTHONY *see* **ANTONY**

ANTOINETTE *see* **ANTONY**

ANTONIA *see* **ANTONY**

ANTONY *m.* (*an'teni*)

from the name of a Roman clan. Its most famous member was Marcus Antonius, the Mark Antony of Shakespeare's *Julius Caesar* and *Antony and Cleopatra*. The name was very popular in the Middle Ages as a result of the influence of St. Antony the Great and St. Antony of Padua. The alternative spelling, Anthony, was introduced after the Renaissance, when it was assumed that the name was derived from the Greek *anthos*, meaning 'flower'. The usual short form is Tony, which is also used for the feminine forms Antonia and Antoinette. A feminine short form, Toni, is also found, as are Toinette, Net and Nettie, from Antoinette.

AOIFFE *see* **EVE**

AONGHUS *see* **AENEAS, ANGUS**

APRIL *f.* (*ā'pril*)

from the name of the month. Like June (q.v.) it has been used as a girl's name in the 20th century.

ARABEL *see* **ARABELLA**

ARABELLA *f.* (*arĕbel'ę*)

a possible variant of Amabel (q.v.), though it could be derived from the Latin for 'obliging'. It has been widely used in Scotland in the forms Arabel and Arabella. There was also a rare form, Arbell, but this has disappeared, and even Arabella is now rarely found.

ARBELL *see* ARABELLA

ARCHIBALD *m.* (*à'chibawld*)

from the Old German words meaning 'true' and 'bold'. The Old English form was used in East Anglia before the Norman Conquest and also appears with Norman connections in Domesday Book. Thereafter it became primarily Scottish, and was associated particularly with the Douglas and Campbell families. The most usual diminutive is Archie.

ARCHIE *see* ARCHIBALD

ARIADNE *f.* (*ariad'ni*)

This is a Greek name of obscure origin. In Greek mythology Ariadne was the daughter of King Minos of ancient Crete. She helped Theseus to escape from the labyrinth by giving him a thread to mark his way. The name has been used occasionally in Britain in the 20th century.

ARLEEN, ARLINE *see* ALINE

ARMEL *m.* (*àmẹl'*)

This is the name of a Breton saint, and it is found very rarely in Britain.

ARMINEL *m.* (*à'minẹl*)

This name is probably derived from the Old German meaning 'soldier'. Armin, an English form of the French Armand, is found in the 17th and 18th centuries, and Arminel may be a diminutive of this. The latter seems to have been confined to the West Country where it survives to this day.

ARNOLD *m.* (*à'nẹld*)

from the Old German for 'eagle' and 'power'. It appeared in various forms, both Germanic and French, in the Middle Ages, and dropped out of use between the 17th and 19th centuries.

It survived as a surname and this may have helped it to regain its present popularity.

ARTEMISIA f. (àtęmēz'ię)

from the Greek meaning 'belonging to Artemis'. Artemis was the Greek goddess of wild animals, vegetation, childbirth and the hunt, comparable to the Roman Diana. Artemisia was the name of the Queen of Caria in the 4th century B.C., who built the Mausoleum at Halicarnassus for her husband. She was also celebrated as a botanist and medical researcher. The name was first used in Britain in the 18th century and still survives in some families.

ARTHUR m. (à'thę)

The origin of this name is disputed. Possible sources are the Welsh word for 'bear', the Irish word meaning 'stone', and the Roman clan name 'Artorius'. The first mention of the British hero, King Arthur, is in the 8th century *Historia Britonum* of Nennius. Between the 13th and 16th centuries the name was spelt Artur. There was a revival of the name in the 19th century when Queen Victoria's younger son was the second Prince Arthur. The first was the elder son of Henry VII.

ARTUR *see* **ARTHUR**

ASPASIA *f.* (*aspā′ ziẹ*)

from the Greek for 'welcome'. This name occurs in a play called *The Maid's Tragedy* by Beaumont and Fletcher, which was first performed in 1611. The name was used very occasionally thereafter.

ASTRID *f.* (*as′trid*)

from the Old German words meaning 'god' and 'strength'. The name of the wife of St. Olaf of Norway, it has long been popular in Scandinavia, and has been used in Britain in the 20th century. Its popularity was no doubt increased by the much loved Belgian queen Astrid, who died in a motor accident in 1935.

ATHALWOLF see **ADOLPHUS**

ATHENE f. (*athē′nē*)

This is the name of the Greek goddess of war and peace, and in Roman times, of wisdom. It has been used occasionally as a girl's name in Britain.

AUBERON see **AUBREY**

AUBERT see **ALBERT**

AUBREY m. (*aw′bri*)

from the Old German meaning 'elf' and 'ruler'. In medieval romance the diminutive Auberon was used, and Shakespeare adopted it in the variant form Oberon, for *A Midsummer Night's Dream*. The German form Alberic developed first into Albery and later into Aubrey, which has survived as a boy's name, though not a common one.

AUDREY f. (*aw′dri*)

the short form of Etheldreda, from the Old English for 'noble' and 'strength'. It first appears in written form in the

16th century, and was used mostly by country folk until the late 19th century, when it came into general use.

AUGUSTA *see* AUGUSTUS

AUGUSTINE, AUSTIN *m.* (*awgus'tin, os'tin*)

from a diminutive of Latin Augustus, meaning 'venerable'. The shortened form, Austin, was very popular in the Middle Ages on account of St. Augustine, the first Archbishop of Canterbury. Though better known as a surname it is still used as a personal name. Augustine was revived in the 19th century by the Oxford Movement and has remained in use since (*see* AUGUSTUS).

AUGUSTUS *m.* (*awgus'tẹs*)

from the Latin for 'venerable'. It was adopted as a title by some of the German princes after the Renaissance, and was introduced to Britain as a Christian name by the Hanoverians. In the early 19th century it was also popular in the feminine form, Augusta, with the pet forms Gus and Gussie (*see* AUGUSTINE).

AURELIA *f.* (*awrē'lię*)

from the Latin for 'gold'. It has been used occasionally since the 17th century, and recently a short form, Auriol, has appeared.

AURIOL *see* AURELIA

AURORA *f.* (*awraw'rę*)

from the Latin name of the goddess of the dawn. It was introduced into Britain at the time of the Renaissance. It has often been used in poetic contexts as in Browning's *Aurora Leigh*.

AVERELL *see* AVERIL

AVERIL *f. and m.* (*ā'veril*)

probably from the Old English for 'boar' and 'battle', which appears as Everild in the 7th century. It was regularly in use until the 17th century, since when it has been rather rare. Averell Harriman, the American states-man, shows a variant form, which has been used as a masculine name in

North America at least. The modern form Averil is often confused with Avril (q.v.).

AVERY see ALFRED

AVICE see AVIS

AVIS f. (ā′vis)

The origin of this name, which was popular in England in the Middle Ages, is obscure. It occurred only rarely between the 16th and 19th centuries and was sometimes spelt Avice. It is still a rather uncommon name.

AVRIL f. (av′ril)

from the French for 'April'. The name has become popular in the 20th century, mainly for girls born in April (see AVERIL).

AYLMER m. (āl′me̞)

from the Old English Aethelmaer, meaning 'noble' and 'famous'. The name was common before the Norman Conquest. It was reinforced when the Normans introduced Ailemar, a derivative of an

Old German name. Aylmer became the usual medieval form and it is still used occasionally, although it is more common as a surname.

AYLWIN m. (*āl'win*)

from the Old English meaning 'good (or noble) friend'. The name survived the Norman Conquest and is still in use, though it has never been common. (*see* ALVIN).

B

BAB, BABS *see* **BARBARA**

BABETTE *see* **ELIZABETH**

BALDWIN m. (*bawld'win*)

from the Old German meaning 'brave friend'. It is found in Old English, and was very popular in the early Middle Ages. It is now rare, but the surnames Baldin, Bodkin and Bowden, which are derived from it, are still common.

BARBARA *f.* (*bà'brę*)

from the Greek word meaning 'strange' or 'foreign', and associated with St. Barbara, a 3rd century martyr. The name was little used after the Reformation, but in the 20th century it became very popular again. Abbreviations include Bab and Babs. The variant form Barbra has recently become popular.

BARBRA *see* **BARBARA**

BARDOLPH *m.* (*bà'dolf*)

from the Old German meaning 'bright wolf'. It is now rather rare, although it survives in the surnames Bardolph and Bardell. The short form is Bardy.

BARDY *see* **BARDOLPH**

BARNABAS *m.* (*bà'nębęs*)

from the Hebrew meaning 'son of exhortation or consolation', and best known as the name bestowed upon the New Testament companion of St. Paul. The diminutive, Barnaby, was popular in the 19th century, when Dickens wrote a novel called *Barnaby Rudge*. The name is having a revival now, together with its short form, Barney, which it shares with Bernard.

BARNABY *see* **BARNABAS**

BARNEY *see* **BARNABAS, BERNARD**

BARRY *m.* (*bar'i*)

from the Irish for 'spear'. For a long time it remained an exclusively Irish name, associated with an Irish saint. It is also the name of a Welsh hermit, who gave his name to Barry Island. It is now in general use.

BART, BAT *see* **BARTHOLOMEW**

BARTHOLOMEW *m.* (*bàthol'ĕmū*)

from the Hebrew meaning 'son of Talmai', surname of the Apostle Nathanael. It was very popular in the Middle Ages when the cult of St. Bartholomew was at its height. St. Bartholomew's hospital in London was founded in the 12th century and an annual Bartholomew Fair was held in London to provide funds for it which was only suppressed in the 19th century. The name is still in use, with its short forms Bart and Bat.

BAS, BASIE *see* BASIL

BASIL *m.* (*baz'el*)

from the Greek meaning 'kingly'. It was probably brought to England by the Crusaders, and it has remained in use ever since. Diminutives include Bas and Basie, and there are two feminine forms, Basilia and Basilie. These were common in the Middle Ages, but are hardly ever found today.

BASILIA, BASILIE *see* BASIL

BASTIAN, BASTIEN
see SEBASTIAN

BEA, BEATTY *see* BEATRICE

BEATA *f.* (*bē'ta, bēā'tē*)

from the Latin meaning 'blessed 'or 'happy'. Originally a name in its own right, it is now used occasionally as a pet form of Beatrice (q.v.).

BEATRICE f. (bĕ′ę̄tris)

from the Latin Beatrix, meaning 'bringer of happiness'. It has strong literary associations. Dante's Beatrice is probably the best known, but Shakespeare also used the name in *Much Ado About Nothing*. In the form Beatrix, the name is remembered for the writer of Children's stories, Beatrix Potter. Short forms include Bea, Beatty and Trixie. There is also a Welsh variant, Bettrys.

BEATRIX see BEATRICE

BECKY see REBECCA

BEL see BELINDA

BEL, BELLA, BELLE see ANNABEL, ISABEL

BELINDA f. (bęlin′dę)

from an Old German compound word, the latter part of which means 'a snake' (see LINDA). Its popular use began in the 18th century when it was used in plays by Congreve and Vanbrugh, and in

Pope's poem *The Rape of the Lock*. Short forms include Bel, Linda and Lindy.

BEN, BENNY *see* BENJAMIN

BENEDICK *see* BENEDICT

BENEDICT *m.* (*ben'edict*)

from the Latin meaning 'blessed', and most familiar as the name of St. Benedict, founder of the Benedictine Order. It was common in medieval England in the forms Bennet and Benedick. The latter is the name of a character in Shakespeare's *Much Ado About Nothing*. There is a feminine form Benedicta, but the Spanish-American Benita is more common.

BENEDICTA *see* BENEDICT

BENITA *see* BENEDICT

BENJAMIN *m.* (*ben'jemin*)

from the Hebrew meaning 'son of the south' or 'right hand', which might imply 'son of strength'. The Old Testament story of Benjamin, son of Jacob, gave the name the added implications of a favoured, youngest son. The commonest pet forms are Ben and Benny, although Benjy is also found.

BENJY *see* **BENJAMIN**

BENNET *see* **BENEDICT**

BERENICE *f.* (*berenēs'*)

from the Greek meaning 'bringer of victory'. It was spread by the imperial conquests of Alexander the Great over Europe and Asia. It was especially popular in Egypt, during the period of Macedonian rule, and its use spread also to the family of Herod of Judea. It is still popular, in its modern form Bernice, among Jewish families.

BERNADETTE *f.* (*benedet'*)

from the French diminutive of Bernard (q.v.). It has been used regularly in Britain, due to the influence of St. Bernadette of Lourdes, who lived in the mid 19th century.

BERNADINE *see* **BERNARD**

BERNARD *m.* (*bẹ′nẹd*)

from the Old German and Old English compound of 'bear' and 'hard', implying strength and courage. It was very popular in the Middle Ages. Two important saints having the name were St. Bernard of Menthon, after whom St. Bernard dogs are named, and St. Bernard of Clairvaux who inspired the Second Crusade. It has remained in use ever since. In addition to Bernadette (q.v.), there is another feminine form, Bernadine. The most usual short forms are Bernie and Barney.

BERNICE *see* BERENICE

BERRY *see* BERTRAM

BERT, BERTIE *see* ALBERT, BERTRAM, BERTRAND, GILBERT, HERBERT, ROBERT

BERTA *see* BERTHA

BERTHA *f.* (*bẹr′thẹ*)

from the old German word meaning 'bright'. The first famous English Bertha was the wife of King Ethelbert of Kent who welcomed St. Augustine to England. In the Middle Ages both Bertha and Berta were popular, and the name has been regularly used since, although it is rather uncommon at present.

BERTRAM *m.* (*ber'trem*)

from the Old German words meaning 'bright' and 'raven', the bird associated with the god Odin. The name has been used in England since the early Middle Ages, and has the diminutives Bert and Bertie, and the less common Berry.

BERTRAND *m.* (*ber'trend*)

the French form of Bertram (q.v.), now used in Britain as a name in its own right. It shares the diminutives Bert and Bertie with Bertram.

BERYL *f.* (*ber'il*)

from the gem, beryl, the name of which is related to the Arabic for crystal. It did not appear before the 19th century, but has been popular in the early and middle 20th century.

BESS, BESSIE *see* **ELIZABETH**

BETH *see* **ELIZABETH**

BETHANY *f.* (*beth'ĕni*)

This is a rather rare girl's name taken from a New Testament place name, the village where Lazarus lived.

BETHIA *f.* (*bĕ'thiĕ*)

from the Hebrew for 'daughter of the Lord'. This name occurs in the Authorised Version of the Old Testament (1 Chronicles IV.18) as Bithiah, but the Latin Vulgate gives it as Bethia. The name was most popular in Scotland in the 17th century but is now very rare. The short form is Beth, shared with Elizabeth.

BETSY, BETTY *see* **ELIZABETH**

BETTINA *f.* (*betē'nĕ*)

a name probably contrived by adding a diminutive suffix to one of the short forms of Elizabeth (q.v.).

BETTRYS *see* **BEATRICE**

BEVERL(E)Y *m. and f.* (*bev'eli*)

from the Old English meaning 'of the beaver-meadow'. This name survives as a surname and Christian name both in Britain and North America.

BEVIS *m.* (*bev'is*)

This is a French name introduced into England by the Norman Conquest. It has been rarely used since, although a novel by Richard Jeffries published in 1882 was called *Bevis, the Story of a Boy*, and this may have resulted in a slight revival.

BIANCA *see* **BLANCHE**

BIDDY *see* **BRIDGET**

BILL, BILLIE *see* **WILLIAM**

BLAISE *m.* (*blāz*)

from French, meaning either one who comes from the region of Blois, or, derived from Latin, 'stammerer'. It is also spelled Blase and Blaze.

BLANCHE *f.* (*blànsh*)

This is a popular French name which was brought to England in the 13th century. It means 'white' or 'fair-skinned'. The Italian form Bianca was used by Shakespeare, and both are still found occasionally.

BLASE, BLAZE *see* **BLAISE**

BLODWEN *f.* (*blod'win*)

This is a Welsh name meaning 'white flower', and rarely found outside Wales.

BOB, BOBBIE *see* **ROBERT**

BONAMY *m.* (*bon'ami*)

from the French meaning 'good friend'. It is a rare name in Britain, but is common as a surname in France.

BONNY *f.* (*bon'i*)

This is very often used as a nickname but it may have its origin in the Latin *bona*, meaning 'good', which was used in the Middle Ages.

BORIS _m._ (_bor'is_)

from the Russian word for 'fight'. It has been used occasionally in Britain and North America in the 20th century, possibly due to cultural influences such as Moussorgsky's opera about the Tsar Boris Godunov, the film actor Boris Karloff, and lately, perhaps the Russian author of _Dr. Zhivago_, Boris Pasternak.

BRAM _see_ **ABRAHAM**

BRAND _see_ **BRENDA**

BRANWEN _f._ (_bran'wen_)

from the Welsh meaning 'beautiful raven'. This name is associated with a legend in _Mabinogion_ and with the story of Tristan and Iseult. It is still in use in Wales.

BRENDA _f._ (_bren'de_)

probably a feminine form of the Norseman's name Brand, meaning 'a sword', found in the Shetlands and used by Scott in his novel _The Pirate_. It has been used regularly since the 19th century.

BRENDAN *m.* (*bren'den*)

from the name of the 6th century Irish saint credited in legend with the discovery of America. It is still in use today, mainly in Ireland, with rare examples in Scotland.

BRIAN *m.* (*brī'en*)

a Celtic name, the origin of which is obscure, though it may be derived from words meaning 'hill' and 'strength'. It was known mainly in Celtic areas until the Norman Conquest, when it was introduced to England. Brian Boru, sometimes spelt Brien, was a famous Irish King of the 11th century. The name continued to be popular in England until Tudor times, but after that it disappeared until it was reintroduced from Ireland in the 18th century. Today the spelling Bryan is also found.

BRIDE, BRIDIE *see* **BRIDGET**

BRIDGET *f.* (*brij'it*)

This may be derived either from a Celtic

goddess whose name meant 'strength' and from the 5th century Irish saint, Bridget, or from a 14th century saint Brigitto, whose name meant 'mountain protection'. The Irish name also appears in the forms Brigid, Brigit and Bride, with the diminutives Bridie and Biddy.

BRIGID, BRIGIT *see* **BRIDGET**

BRIGITTO *see* **BRIDGET**

BRISEIDA *see* **CRESSIDA**

BRONWEN *f.* (*bron'win*)

from the Welsh words meaning 'white breast'. This name has long been popular in Wales and is surrounded by ancient legend.

BRUCE *m.* (*brôôs*)

A Scottish surname which came to Britain at the time of the Norman Conquest. It derives from the name of the village of Brieuse in Normandy. A member of this family, Robert Bruce, became King of Scotland, and was the ancestor of the Stuart Kings. It has only been used as a Christian name since the 19th century, although it is now popular both in Scotland and England. Brucie is a rare feminine form, which is also a masculine pet form.

BRUCIE *see* BRUCE

BRUNELLA, BRUNETTA *f.*
(broŏnel'<u>e</u>, broŏnet'<u>e</u>)

These rare feminine names are derived respectively from Old French and modern Italian, both meaning 'dark-haired'.

BRUNO *m.* (broŏ'nō)

This is a rather uncommon name from the Old English for 'brown'. It was used in England before the Norman Conquest. Many Browns, however, derive their surnames from the Norman French nickname, le brun.

BRYAN *see* BRIAN

BRYONY *f.* (brī'ŏni)

This is one of the more uncommon girls' names taken from plant and flower names.

C

CADDY *see* **CAROLINE**

CADWALLADER *m.* *(kadwol'ĕdĕ)*

from the Welsh meaning 'battle chief', and one of a series of names with the Welsh word for battle as the root (see CHAD). It is found in Wales and in North America.

CALEB *m.* *(kā'leb)*

from the Hebrew meaning 'intrepid' or 'dog'. First appearing in the 16th century, it is now usually found in North America and Scotland.

CALVIN *m.* *(kal'vin)*

from the surname of the 16th century French religious reformer Jean Cauvin or Chauvin, latinised to Calvinus, and adopted as a Christian name by Protestants. It may be derived from the Old French meaning 'bald'. It is most commonly found in North America and Scotland.

CAMERON m. (kam'eren)

from the Gaelic meaning 'crooked nose'. It is the name of a famous Scottish clan, and its use as a Christian name is mainly confined to Scotland.

CAMILLA f. (kemil'e)

a Latin name, attributed by the Latin poet Virgil (1st century B.C.), to a queen of the Volsci tribe, and therefore possibly of Etruscan origin. It was first recorded in Britain in 1205. The 18th century novel *Camilla* by Madame D'Arblay may have increased its popularity, as may Greta Garbo's film role as *Camille* in the 20th century, but it has never been common.

CAMILLE see CAMILLA

CANDIDA f. (kan'dide)

from the Latin meaning 'white'. It was the name of several saints, amongst them one from Naples whom St. Paul is said to have cured. The name was not used in Britain until the early 20th century and its introduction was probably effected by G. B. Shaw's play *Candida* and its heroine.

CARA *f.* (*kä'rẹ*)

This is probably the Italian word meaning 'dear', which has been given as a Christian name in Britain in the 20th century. Another possible source is the Irish meaning 'friend'. There is also a variant Carita, derived from the Latin meaning 'beloved'.

CARADOC *m.* (*kẹrad'ok*)

from the Welsh meaning 'beloved'. It is common in Wales, but not in any other part of Britain.

CARL, KARL *m.* (*kàl*)

Karl is the German form of Charles. The name has spread into general use in America, and from there into Britain, probably only in the 20th century.

CARLA *see* CAROLINE

CARLO *see* CAROLINE

CARLOTTA *see* CHARLOTTE, LOLA

CARMEL *f.* *(kảʹmẹl)*

from the Hebrew meaning 'garden', and the name of a famous mountain near the city of Haifa in Israel. St. Louis is said to have founded the church and convent on this mountain which, as legend has it, the Virgin Mary and infant Jesus often visited. Its use as a Christian name is restricted to Roman Catholics. Variant forms are Carmela and Carmelita.

CARMELA, CARMELITA
see **CARMEL**

CARMEN *f.* *(kảʹmen)*

This is probably the Latin for 'song'. It may also have some connection with the Hebrew for 'garden' (*see* CARMEL). Borrowed from Spain, this name has been used occasionally in Britain since Bizet's opera *Carmen* became popular (first performance 1875). Charmaine *(shảmān')* is a French equivalent which is also occasionally found.

CAROL m. *(kar'ĕl)*

possibly from the Irish Cathal, and certainly an anglicised form of the Latin Carolus and Slav Karel. Its use has spread to Britain from North America but it is not very common.

CAROL, CAROLA, CAROLINA *see* **CAROLINE**

CAROLINE, CAROLYN f. *(kar'ĕlin, kar'ĕlin)*

from the Italian feminine form of Carlo, the equivalent of Charles, which was introduced into Britain from Southern Germany by Queen Caroline of Brandenburg-Anspach, wife of George II. It has been very popular since the 18th century. Derivatives are Carla, Carol, Carola, Carolina. Abbreviations include Carrie, Caddy, and Lyn.

CAROLUS *see* **CAROL, CHARLES**

CARRIE *see* **CAROLINE**

CASPAR *see* **JASPER**

CASS, CASSIE *see* **CASSANDRA**

CASSANDRA *f.* (*kęsàn'drę*)

In Greek literature this was the name of a prophetic princess of Troy. It first became popular in the Middle Ages with the revival of classical learning and the sympathy which the fate of Troy aroused. The name has continued in use ever since. It is perhaps best known in Britain as the pseudonym of a popular journalist. Also found are Cassandry and abbreviations Cassie and Cass. The latter also occurs as a masculine name.

CASSANDRY *see* **CASSANDRA**

CATHAL *see* **CAROL**

CATHERINE, CATHARINE *see* **KATHARINE**

CATHY *see* **KATHARINE**

CATRIONA *f.* (*katrē'ōnę*)

the Gaelic form of Katharine (q.v.). It was the title of a book by Robert Louis Stevenson, and became very popular in the 19th century as a result of this. It is quite common in Scotland today.

CECIL, CECILY, CICELY
see CECILIA

CECIL *m.* (*ses'il*)

from the Latin meaning 'blind'. It was the name of a famous Roman clan and was first adopted into English as a girl's name. The popularity of the name in its masculine form only became marked in the 19th century, probably as a result of the influence of the Cecil family. Among the famous members of this family were Lord Burghley, advisor to Queen Elizabeth I, and his son Robert Cecil, whom James I created Earl of Salisbury.

CECILIA *f.* (*sesē'liε*)

from the Latin meaning 'blind', and the name of the 2nd century martyr and saint, popularly regarded as the patroness of music. The name was first introduced into Britain by the Normans. Variant forms of the name are Cicely, Cecily, Sisley, Cecil. The popular shortened form Celia probably came into vogue as a result of the character of that name in Shakespeare's play *As You Like It*. Other abbreviated forms are Sis, Ciss and Cissy (*see* SHEILA).

CEDRIC *m.* (*sed'rik*)

from Sir Walter Scott's character in the novel *Ivanhoe*. Scott is said to have mistaken it for Cerdic, who was the founder and the first king of West Saxony. Cedric became popular as a result of the book *Little Lord Fauntleroy* by F. H. Burnett (1886), whose hero bore that name. It is a fairly common name in Britain today.

CELESTE *f.* (*selest'*)

from the Latin meaning 'heavenly'. This name and its diminutive Celestine are most common in France, where the influence of the 13th century saint, Celestine, may have been greater than in Britain. Celestine has been used in Britain as a masculine name to transliterate the Gaelic Gilleasbuig, also rendered as Gillespie (q.v.).

CELESTINE *see* **CELESTE**

CELIA *see* **CECILIA**

CELINA, CÉLINE *see* **SELINA**

CENYDD *see* **KENNETH**

CERDIC *see* **CEDRIC**

CERIDWEN, KERRIDWEN *f.*
(*kerid'wen*)

from Welsh. It was the name of a Celtic goddess who was said to inspire poetry. Its use is confined to Wales.

CHAD *m.* (*chad*)

from the Welsh meaning 'battle' or 'defence', and the name of a 7th century saint who was Bishop of Lichfield. The name has become fairly popular in America in the 20th century. A famous holder of the name today is the Rev. Chad Varah, founder of the Samaritan organisation, which helps those in despair.

CHARIS *f.* (*kar'is*)

from the Greek meaning 'grace'. It

was first used as a Christian name in the 17th century, although the 16th century poet Edmund Spenser used the name Charissa in his *Faerie Queen*. The name has never been popular in Britain.

CHARISSA *see* CHARIS

CHARITY *f.* (char'iti)

from the Latin *caritas*, meaning 'Christian love'. Translated into English as charity, the name was adopted when it became the custom for Puritans to name each child after one of the Christian virtues. In the 16th century John Bunyan used the name Charity for one of the characters in his *Pilgrim's Progress*. In Dickens' novel *Martin Chuzzlewit*, the name Charity is shortened to Cherry, and this is still a common form. Another abbreviation is Chattie, used also for Charlotte.

CHARLES *m.* (châls)

originally from Old German carl or Old English *ceorl*, meaning 'man'. It was latinised as Carolus and later adapted by the French to Charles (*shàl*). In France the name was very popular during the Middle Ages due to the fame of the Emperor Charles the Great or Charlemagne. The Normans brought the name to England in the 12th century, but it did not become popular until its use by the Royal House of Stuart caused it to be taken up by Royalists in the 17th century and Jacobites in the 18th century. Its popularity has continued to increase ever since, especially in the abbreviated form Charlie.

CHARLIE *see* CHARLES, CHARLOTTE

CHARLOTTE *f.* (*shà'lẹt*)

the French feminine form of Charles. It was introduced into Britain from France in the early 17th century. George III's wife, Charlotte Sophia of Mecklenburg-Strelitz, popularised the name. Goethe's heroine from the novel *The Sorrows of Werther*, and Princess Charlotte, daughter of George IV, increased the name's popularity.

In the 20th century the name is less often found. Carlotta is the Italian form. Abbreviations are Lottie, Lotty, Totty and occasionally Charlie.

CHARMIAN f. (kǎ′mien, shǎ′mien)

from the Greek meaning 'joy'. Charmian was the name of one of Cleopatra's attendants. Shakespeare's *Antony and Cleopatra* gave the name a wider public, and in the 17th century Dryden used it again in his play on the same subject, *All for Love*. The name has never been widely used.

CHATTIE see CHARITY

CHERRY see CHARITY

CHLODOWIG see LEWIS

CHLOE f. (klō′i)

from the Greek meaning 'a green shoot', a name given to the goddess Demeter who protected the green fields, In classical literature it was a pastoral name which was echoed by Elizabethan poets. It was adopted by American

Negroes from the New Testament story of the woman of Corinth whom St. Paul converted, and is still in use.

CHRIS, CHRISSY *see* CHRISTABEL, CHRISTIANA, CHRISTY, CHRISTOPHER

CHRISTABEL *f. (kris′tebel)*

This Christian name was first used in Britain in the 16th century, and is thought to be a combination of the Latin words Christus and *bella*, meaning 'beautiful Christian'. It was the name of a character in Middle English literature, and was used by Thomas Percy in his *Ballad of Sir Cauline*. It was probably from this source that the 19th century poet Coleridge took the name of his heroine, in the poem *Christabel*. It is not a common name in Britain. Abbreviated forms are Chris, Chrissy and Christy.

CHRISTEN *see* CHRISTIANA

CHRISTIAN *f. and m. (kris′tien)*

from the Latin meaning 'Christian'.

It has been used in Britain since the 13th century. It became more popular after its use by Bunyan for the hero of *Pilgrim's Progress*, but never has been as common as the feminine form Christiana (q.v.).

CHRISTIANA *f.* (*kristià'ne̦*)

from the Latin meaning 'a Christian'. The name was introduced into Britain in the 13th century, although the word was not commonly used as a noun or adjective until the 16th century. The Old English word, Christen, was in common use before then, but the names Christina and Christine which derive from it were not popular, though they are now the commonest forms. The pet name Kirsty is still found in Scotland. Abbreviations are Chrissy and Chris.

CHRISTINA, CHRISTINE
see **CHRISTIANA**

CHRISTMAS *m. and f.* (*kris'me̦s*)

taken from the church festival and used to commemorate the birth of a child on

Christmas Day. The name has been in use since at least the 13th century, although it has never been common. A much more popular equivalent is Noel (q.v.). A well-known holder of the name is Mr. Christmas Humphreys, the President of the London Buddhist Society.

CHRISTOPHER m. (*kris'tefe*)

from the Greek meaning 'bearing Christ', and used originally to describe all Christians. It was first used as a Christian name by the early Christian saint who was believed to have carried the infant Christ to safety across a river. Thus St. Christopher became the patron saint of travellers, and the name became common in Roman Catholic countries. The popularity of the name in Britain has fluctuated since the 13th century when it was first used, but it is now fairly common. The Scottish equivalent of the name was Chrystal or Crystal. Abbreviated forms are Kester, Kit, Chris and Christie.

CHRYSEIDA, CRISEYDE
see **CRESSIDA**

CHRYSTAL, CRYSTAL
see **CHRISTOPHER**

CICELY *see* **CECILIA**

CIMMIE *see* **CYNTHIA**

CINDERELLA *f.* (*sinderel'ĕ*)

from the French meaning 'little one of the ashes'. It is the name of the fairy tale heroine who left her drudgery by the hearthside to marry a prince. Cindy is the short form which it shares with Lucinda (q.v.).

CINDY *see* **CINDERELLA, LUCINDA**

CISS, CISSY *see* **CECILIA**

CLAIRE *see* **CLARA**

CLARA, CLARE *f.* (*klē'rĕ, klēr*)

from the Latin meaning 'clear' or 'famous'. This name first appeared in the 13th century as Clare. The Italian religious order of the Sisters of St. Clara, or 'Poor Clares', founded in the

13th century, was probably responsible for the rapid spread of the name throughout Europe. A variant form is the French Claire, popularised by the British film actress Claire Bloom. Among the many derivatives are Claribel and Clarinda. An abbreviated form is Clarrie.

CLARENCE *m.* (*klar'ens*)

This name stems from the dukedom created in the 14th century for the English king Edward III's son, Lionel, who had married the heiress of Clare in Suffolk (*see* CLARE). It was first used as a Christian name in the early 19th century in Maria Edgeworth's novel *Helen*. It has never been widely used.

CLARIBEL *f.* (*klar'ibel*)

the name of the Queen of Tunis in Shakespeare's play *The Tempest*. A derivative of Clara (q.v.), the name has never been widely used.

CLARICE *f.* (*klar'is*)

from the Latin meaning 'making famous'. The name spread to England from France. The variant form Clarissa was made popular in the 18th century by Samuel Richardson's novel *Clarissa Harlowe*, but it did not achieve lasting popularity. It shares the abbreviation Clarrie with Clara.

CLARINDA *see* CLARA

CLARISSA *see* CLARICE

CLARRIE *see* CLARA, CLARICE

CLAUD(E) *m.* (*klawd*)

from the name of the Roman clan Claudius, derived from the Latin meaning 'lame', or the Greek meaning 'famous'. In homage to the Emperor Claudius, under whom Britain was conquered by the Romans, the name was used for both men and women in the 1st and 2nd centuries. Its use soon lapsed in Britain though not in France, and it was from the French that it was taken and revived in Britain in the 16th century by the Scottish family of Hamilton. Lord Claud Hamilton had several French connections. The name is still fairly uncommon. A derivative is Claudian, and the pet form Claudie is sometimes found.

CLAUDIA *f.* (*klaw'diẹ*)

from the Latin family name Claudius and the masculine Claud (q.v.). It is unusual in Britain, though very popular in France. It has been suggested that the name may have connections with the Welsh Gladys (q.v.).

CLAUDIAN, CLAUDIE *see* CLAUD

CLAUDIUS *see* CLAUD

CLAUS *see* NICHOLAS

CLEM, CLEMMIE *see* CLEMENT, CLEMENTINA

CLEMENCE, CLEMENCY *f.*
(*klem'ẹns, klem'ẹnsi*)

from the Latin meaning 'mildness'. The name first appeared in Britain in the 13th century. It is not a common Christian name.

CLEMENT *m.* *(klem'ent)*

from the Latin meaning 'mild' or 'merciful'. It was the name of an early saint and of several popes. It was popular in Britain from the 12th century until the time of the Reformation, and had a revival in the reign of Queen Victoria. The Christian name was the origin of many surnames, including Clements, Clemens and Clemson. It has become more popular since the 19th century. Its abbreviated forms are Clem and Clemmie.

CLEMENTINA, CLEMENTINE *f.*
(klementē'ne, klem'entīn)

from the masculine name Clement (q.v.), It was originally a German adaptation and was most popular during the 19th century. It is rarely used today, except in the well-known song about the Californian Gold Rush in 1849. The best known example of the name today is Lady Spencer Churchill, wife of the late Sir Winston Churchill.

CLEO f. (klē′ō)

from the Greek meaning 'glory', or
'father's fame'. It is a shortened form
of Cleopatra. The famous Egyptian
queen holding this name died in 30 B.C.
She has been commemorated in many
great works of English literature. Probably
Shakespeare's play *Antony and Cleopatra*
has been most influential in spreading
the use of the name.

CLEOPATRA *see* CLEO

CLIFF *see* CLIFFORD

CLIFFORD m. (klif′ęd)

from the place name, Clifford, of which
there are several in Britain. It was
used as a surname until the end of the
19th century when it became known as
a Christian name. It is not common
in Britain today. Its abbreviated form
is Cliff.

CLIVE m. (klīv)

This name is possibly derived from a
village in Shropshire and connected

with the word 'cliff'. The name was first used as a Christian name by the 19th century novelist Thackeray for a character in his book *The Newcomes*, and has since been used fairly widely in Britain. Its popularity is largely due to the surname of Robert Clive (Clive of India), especially among families with traditions of service in India.

CLODAGH *f.* (klō′da)

from the name of a river in Ireland. It was first used in the 20th century as a Christian name by the Marquis of Waterford for his daughter. It is in common use only in Ireland.

CLOTILDA *f.* (klōtil′de̦)

from a combination of the Old German words for 'loud' and 'battle'. Clotilda was a queen of France in the 5th and 6th centuries, and she converted her husband, King Clovis, to Christianity. The name is used mostly by Roman Catholics in Britain, but it is not common.

CLOVIS *see* **LEWIS**

COELINA *see* **SELINA**

COIONNEACH *see* **KENNETH**

COLIN *m.* (*kọl'in*)

from the Gaelic meaning 'a young dog' or 'youth'. It is common in Scotland but rarer in England, where it was introduced by way of the French diminutive of Nicholas, which was used in literature as the name of a peasant. The Welsh 'collwyn' has the meaning 'hazel grove'. In Switzerland the name Colin Tampon is used as a national nickname.

COLLEEN *f.* (*kol'ēn*)

from the Irish for 'girl'. The name is not widely used in Britain, but it is fairly common in North America.

COLLETTE *f.* (*kolet'*)

from the French diminutive of Nicole. It was the name of the reformer of the religious order of 'Poor Clares' in the 15th century, and is popular among

Roman Catholics today. The Christian name is the origin of the surnames Colet, Collett, and Colect. The name is best known in this country as the pen-name of a 20th century French writer.

COLUM m. (kol'ĕm)

This name was adopted by the Irish from the Latin meaning 'dove'. It was introduced to Scotland in the 6th century with the arrival of St. Columba, who was also known as Colum Cille, 'Colum of the Church' (see MALCOLM).

COLUM CILLE see COLUM

COLUMBA see COLUM

COMYN m. (kom'in)

This name is used occasionally in Scotland and Ireland, but is more common as a surname. It may derive from the Irish for 'crooked', or from the French surname brought to Britain by the Normans.

CONAN *m.* (*kō'nen*)

from the Irish meaning 'high' or 'wisdom'. It was the name of an early Bishop of London. One of the several saints who bore this name is believed to have been an ancestor of the Dukes of Brittany. The name was introduced to England at the time of the Norman Conquest, and was the origin of the surnames Conan, Connant, Connand, Connon and Conning. It was popular from the 12th to 16th centuries but is not common in Britain today. The most famous holder of the name was Sir Arthur Conan Doyle, creator of the fictional detective, Sherlock Holmes.

CONNAIRE *see* **CONNOR**

CONNIE *see* **CONSTANCE**

CONNOR, CONOR *m.* (*kon'e*)

from the Irish meaning 'strength', 'desire' and possibly 'hound of slaughter'. It was much used in Irish mythology. It is more common as a surname The Irish form is Connaire.

CONRAD *m.* (kon'rad)

from a compound of the Old German words for 'bold' and 'counsel'. The name is found mostly in Germany where the 13th century Duke Conrad was a greatly beloved figure. His public execution by the conquering Charles of Anjou led to a widespread use of this name in German speaking states. Examples of it have been found in Britain since the 15th century. The Old English form is shown in the name of Cenred, King of Mercia. The name has never been common in this country.

CONSTANCE, CONSTANTIA *f.*
(kon'stens, konstant'ie)

from the Latin meaning 'constancy'. The name became popular in many parts of Christendom after Constantine the Great ordered the toleration of Christianity in the Roman Empire, 313 A.D. It was introduced into England at the time of the Norman Conquest, and was adopted by the English as Custance.

The form Constancy was used by the Puritans in the 17th century. Constantia became popular in the 19th century, but today Constance is much more common. Its abbreviation is Connie.

CONSTANCY, CONSTANTIA
see **CONSTANCE**

CONSTANTINE *m.* *(kon'stantīn, kon'stantēn)*

---

from the Latin meaning 'firm'. It was the name of the first Christian Emperor, and so became popular with Christians. Three Scottish kings were named Constantine, after a Cornish saint who was believed to have converted their ancestors to Christianity in the 6th century. It became popular in England from the 12th to the 17th centuries, and was the origin of the surnames Constantine, Considine, Costain and Costin. It is not widely used in Britain today,

CORA *f.* *(kaw'rẹ)*

---

from the Greek word meaning 'girl'. The name did not appear in Britain until the 19th century, although it was already in use in North America. The diminutive Corinna (q.v.) has a much longer record of use.

CORAL *f.* (*kor'el*)

This name reflects the beauty and value of the substance, and has become popular in the 20th century. A French derivative which is also used in Britain is Coralie.

CORALIE *see* CORAL

CORDEILLA *see* CORDELIA

CORDELIA *f.* (*kawdē'liẹ*)

This rather rare name first appeared as Cordeilla in the 16th century chronicles of Holinshed, from which Shakespeare altered the name to Cordelia for his play *King Lear*. The origin is obscure, but Cordula was the Welsh or Cornish name for one of St. Ursula's companions. Kordula and Kordel are the German equivalents.

CORDULA *see* CORDELIA

CORINNA *f. (korin'ę)*

This name is a diminutive of the Greek word meaning 'girl', and a name given to the goddess Persephone, who was associated with the coming of spring. The well-known Greek poetess of the 5th century B.C., who bore the name, probably inspired its popularity among 17th century poets, particularly Herrick. The name did not become common, though the variant form Corinne has been found occasionally (*see* CORA).

CORINNE *see* **CORINNA**

CORMAC *m. (kaw'męk)*

from the Irish meaning 'a charioteer', a name occurring in Irish legend. Through its prevalence in early Irish history and the Irish Church, the name was accepted as having a Christian character in Ireland. A variant is Cormick. It is now more often found as a surname.

CORMICK *see* **CORMAC**

CORNELIA *see* **CORNELIUS**

CORNELIUS m. *(kornēl'iŭs)*

from the Latin word meaning 'horn', and the name of a famous Roman clan. The horn was symbolic of kingship in Roman culture. The name has never been common in Britain. Its abbreviated forms are Corney, Corny, Cornie and Corrie. Cornelia is the feminine form.

CORNEY, CORNIE, CORNY
see **CORNELIUS**

COSIMO *see* **COSMO**

COSMO m. *(koz'mō)*

from the Greek meaning 'order'. It is the name of one of the patron saints of Milan and was used by the famous Italian family of Medici, in the form Cosimo, from the 14th century onwards. It was the name of the 3rd Duke of Gordon who was a friend of Cosimo III, Grand Duke of Tuscany, and the name was introduced into several other Scottish families. It is rather uncommon in Britain today.

CRESSID, CRESSY *see* CRESSIDA

CRESSIDA *f.* (*kres'idǝ*)

Taken from Greek literature, the name
Briseida was used by the 12th century
French playwright Benoit for his faithless
Trojan heroine. It was adapted by the
15th century Italian writer Boccaccio to
Chryseida, in his retelling of the story.
Chaucer used the name Criseyde, and
Shakespeare changed it to Cressida or
Cressid. The name has never been pop-
ular, probably owing to the reputation
for faithlessness which Cressida bears in
English literature. An abbreviated form
is Cressy.

CRISPIN, CRISPIAN, *m.* (*kris'pǝn, kris'piǝn*)

from the Latin meaning 'curled'. The
3rd century martyrs Crispinus and Crispinianus were the patron saints of shoe-
makers. The name was popular in
Britain in the Middle Ages but is
unusual in the 20th century.

CRISPINUS, CRISPINIANUS
see **CRISPIN**

CUDBERT *see* **CUTHBERT**

CUDDY *see* **CUTHBERT**

CUSTANCE *see* **CONSTANCE**

CUTHBERT *m.* (*kuth'bet*)

from the Old English words meaning
'famous' and 'bright'. It was in common
use both before and after the Norman
Conquest, and was the name of the
7th century saint and Bishop of Lindisfarne in Northumbria. It sometimes
appeared as Cudbert, and had the pet
form Cuddy. The name fell out of use
from just after the Reformation until the
19th century, when it was brought back
by the Oxford Movement. It was a
slang term for someone who avoided
military service during the 1914-18
War, and it may be partly due to this
usage that the name is not popular
today.

CY *see* **CYRIL, CYRUS**

CYNTHIA f. (sin'thię)

from one of the titles of the Greek Goddess Artemis, meaning 'of Mount Cynthus'. The name first became known through its use by the Latin poet Propertius, and it was very popular among Elizabethan poets. Mrs. Gaskell's character in her novel *Wives and Daughters* brought it back into favour during the late 19th century, since when it has become fairly common. A pet form sometimes used is Cimmie.

CYPRIAN m. (sip'rięn)

from the Latin Cyprianus, meaning 'from Cyprus'. It was the name of a famous Latin writer, who was a Christian martyr in the 3rd century. The form Cyprianus has also been used occasionally in Britain.

CYRIL m. (sir'ęl)

probably from the Greek meaning 'lord'. There were two saints of this name in the 4th and 5th centuries, and it was a 9th century saint Cyril who took Christianity to the Slavs, and devised the Cyrillic alphabet. The name was first used in England in the 17th century, but did not become common until the 19th century. The name shares its only abbreviation Cy with Cyrus. There is a rare feminine form Cyrilla.

CYRILLA *see* **CYRIL**

CYRO *see* **CYRUS**

CYRUS m. (*sī'rẹs*)

from a Greek form of the Persian word meaning 'sun' or 'throne'. This is the name of the founder of the Persian Empire in the 6th century B.C. It was first used in Britain in the 17th century among Puritans, probably in honour of the fact that the Emperor Cyrus allowed the Jews to return to Palestine from the Babylonian captivity. It is now very popular in North America, where common diminutive forms are Cy and Cyro.

D

DAGMAR *m. and f. (dag'mà)*

a Danish name meaning 'joy of the Dane'. It has spread into North America through Danish immigrant families.

DAI *see* **DAVID**

DAISY *f. (dā'zi)*

a 19th century pet name for Margaret (q.v.) using the English name for the same flower as the French Marguerite. It is sometimes used independently, but is not popular today.

DALE *f. (dāl)*

from the Old English for 'valley'. It is a rare name which has also been used as a masculine name in North America.

DAMARIS *f. (dam'ẹris)*

from the Greek name belonging, in the New Testament, to an Athenian woman converted by St. Paul. Adopted by Puritans in the 17th century, it is very rare today.

DAMHNAIT *see* **DYMPHNA**

DAMIAN *m.* (*dā'miẹn*)

from Greek meaning 'tamer'. There have been four saints called by this name, and it is used almost exclusively by Roman Catholics.

DAMON *m.* (*dā'mẹn*)

from the Greek meaning 'rule' or 'guide'. According to Greek legend, Damon and Pythias were inseparable friends, who were ready to die for each other. It is an unusual name which is perhaps best known through the American writer Damon Runyan.

DAN, DANNY *see* **DANIEL**

DANDY *see* **ANDREW**

DANIEL *m.* (*dan'iẹl*)

the Hebrew name of the Old Testament prophet, meaning 'God has judged'. It is found in England before the Norman Conquest, but only among priests and monks. It became more widespread in the 13th and 14th centuries. The name was revived in the 17th century by Puritans but is now rare, though more common in Ireland and Wales where it is often found as a transliteration of the Irish Domhnall and Welsh Deiniol. Its shortened forms are Dan and Danny, and the feminine Danielle and Daniella are also fairly popular.

DANIELLA, DANIELLE see DANIEL

DANTE m. (dan'te)

an Italian name, famous through the 13th century poet Dante Alighieri. Its use as a given name is rare, and is probably entirely due to the reputation of this poet. The name is an abbreviation of Durante or Durand (q.v.).

DAPHNE f. (daf'ni)

from the Greek for a 'bay' or 'laurel bush.' In classical mythology it was the name of a nymph whom the god Apollo loved. In seeking to escape him she called on the gods for help, and was changed by them into a bush. The name was used mainly for dogs until the turn of the century, when it became quite common as a Christian name. A famous modern example is the novelist Daphne Du Maurier.

DARBY, DERBY *m.* (dà′bi)

The etymology of this name is uncertain. It appears mainly in Ireland and is possibly a shortened form of the Irish Diarm(a)id, meaning 'free man'. It may also derive from the Norse meaning 'deer park'. Darby and Joan, the proverbial name for a loving old couple, probably originated in an 18th century ballad.

D'ARCY *m.* (dà′si)

The English family of this name was founded by Norman d'Areci, one of William the Conqueror's companions. A branch of the family went to Ireland, where Darcy was adopted as a Christian name, possibly to transliterate the Irish Dorchaidh. A variant form is Darsey.

DARREL(L), DARYL *m.* (dar′ẹl)

from the Old English word meaning

'darling'. This name is still very occasionally found.

DARSEY *see* **D'ARCY**

DATHI *see* **DAVID**

DAVE, DAVEY, DAVIE *see* **DAVID**

DAVID *m.* (*dā'vid*)

the Hebrew name of the second king of Israel in the Old Testament, meaning 'beloved'. This name absorbed the Celtic form Dathi and became very popular in Wales and Scotland. The Welsh patron saint is a 6th century David. There were two Scottish kings of this name in the 10th and 14th centuries. The name did not appear in England before the Norman Conquest, but it was a common medieval surname in the variant forms Davy, Davit and Deakin. It has been a common name for centuries and its popularity shows no sign of decreasing. Short forms are Dave, Davy, Davie and in Wales Dai or Taffy, the latter being the common British nickname for a Welshman.

DAVIDA, DAVINA *f.* (*davē'də, davē'nə*)

Scottish feminine forms of David (q.v.), these are found from the 17th century, but are not common.

DAWN *f.* (*dawn*)

This name came into being in the late 19th century. The Latin Aurora (q.v.) had been in vogue slightly earlier, and the English form was probably entirely a literary invention. It has been popular among film stars, and has therefore gained publicity and a fairly large following in recent years.

DEBBIE *see* **DEBORAH**

DEBORAH *f.* (*deb'awrə*)

from Hebrew meaning 'bee', and the name of a prophetess and poet in the Old Testament. It was first used by Puritans in the 17th century. It is not quite so popular today as it formerly was, but is still found fairly often. Debbie is a common abbreviation.

DECIMA *see* DECIMUS

DECIMUS *m.* (*des'imęs*)

Taken from Latin, *decimus*, meaning 'tenth', this was used in Victorian times as a name for the tenth child in large families. Decima was used for girls.

DEINIOL *see* DANIEL

DEIRDRE *f.* (*dēr'dri*)

This is the Irish name of a character in Irish and Scottish legend, possibly meaning 'raging' or 'sorrowful'. Beautiful and wise 'Deirdre of the sorrows', as she is sometimes called, left Ireland in order to marry the man of her choice, and lived with him and his two brothers near Loch Etive. Tempted back to Ireland by a false offer of friendship, the three men were killed, and Deirdre, lamenting her sad lot, committed suicide. The name became popular after the late 19th century Celtic revival.

DELIA *f.* (*dē'lię*)

This name is derived from Delos, the

legendary birthplace of the Greek moon goddess Artemis. It was popular with pastoral poets in the 17th and 18th centuries and is still used occasionally.

DENIS, DENNIS m. (den'is)

a derivation of Dionysos, who was the Greek god of wine and revelry. Denis is the French form and the name of the patron saint of France. It occurs in England from the 12th century on and is very popular today. In Ireland it has long been used as substitute for the Irish Donnchadh. Denise (denēz) is the feminine form, also from French, but it is less common in Britain.

DENISE see DENIS

DENZIL m. (den'zil)

Spelt Denzell, this is an old Cornish family name, possibly cognate with Denis. In the 17th century it came by marriage into the Holles family who adopted it as a Christian name. It is still used by the Holles family and their connections.

DEREK, DERRICK m. *(der'ik)*

a derivation of Old German Theodoric, or 'people's ruler'. It occurs in the 15th century but has only become popular in the last century. Its fall from favour between these two periods is attributed to the notorious 17th century hangman of that name. Variant forms recently revived are Deryk, Deric and the Dutch form Dirk, popularised by the well-known film star Dirk Bogarde. Pet forms are Derry and Rick or Rickie.

DERIC, DERYK *see* **DEREK**

DERMOT m. *(der'mot)*

This is the anglicised spelling of Diarmit, Diarm(a)id, the Irish name meaning 'free from envy', or 'free man'. The legendary character who bore this name eloped with a queen of Tara. He was caught by the husband and forced to hunt a wild boar, thus meeting his death. A shortened form is Darby (q.v.).

DERRY *see* **DEREK**

DÉSIRÉE f. (dāzē′rā)

a French name meaning 'desired'. It has occasionally been borrowed from the French, with the pronunciation retained.

DESMOND m. (dez′mend)

from Irish Deas-Mumhain, meaning 'man of South Munster'. It was originally used as a surname in Ireland. Later it became a Christian name, and came to England in the late 19th century.

DIANA f. (dīan′e)

The Latin name of the Roman goddess equivalent to the Greek Artemis. She was the feminine counterpart of Janus, the sun god, and associated with the moon and virginity. She was also the goddess of hunting and protector of wild animals. Its use as a Christian name dates from the Renaissance, when the French form Diane is also first found. Both names are still popular.

DIANE see **DIANA**

DIARMAID, DIARMID, DIARMIT
see **DARBY, DERMOT**

DICK, DICKE, DICKIE
see **RICHARD**

DICKON *see* **RICHARD**

DILYS *f. (dil'is)*

from the Welsh meaning 'perfect',
'genuine'. The name became current in
Wales in the 19th century, and is now
used throughout Britain. Dilys Powell is
a well-known broadcaster and writer.

DINAH *f. (dī'ne)*

from the Hebrew, meaning 'lawsuit'.
It was the name of one of Jacob's
daughters in the Old Testament. It
came into use in the 17th century
among the Puritans and was a favourite name in the 19th century, when it
was often confused with Diana (q.v.).

DIONYSOS *see* **DENIS**

DIRK *see* **DEREK**

DODIE, DODO *see* **DOROTHEA**

DOLAN *m.* (*dōlen*)

from the Irish meaning 'black-haired'.
It is found more often as a surname in
Britain.

DOLL, DOLLY *see* DOROTHEA

DOLORES *f.* (*dolaw'rez*)

This name was originally a short form
of the Spanish, Maria de Dolores, or
'Mary of the Sorrows', after the feast
of the 'Seven Sorrows of Our Lady'.
This is one of several 'festival' names,
common in Roman Catholic countries.
Mercedes and Noël (q.v.) are two
others occasionally used in Britain.
The name became popular in North
America about 1930. Pet forms are Lola
(q.v.), Lolita and Lo.

DOMHNALL, DOMNALL
see DANIEL, DOMINIC, DONALD

DOMINIC(K) *m.* (*dom'inik*)

from Latin *dominicus*, meaning 'of the
Lord'. It is possible that the name
was first used for children born on the

Sabbath day. It was used in England as a monk's name before the Norman Conquest and probably became more widespread on account of St. Dominic, founder of the Order of Preachers known as the Black Friars (early 13th century). Since the Reformation it has been used almost exclusively by Roman Catholics. In Ireland it is occasionally used as a substitute for the Irish Domhnall. Dominica is a rare feminine form (*see* DONALD).

DOMINICA *see* DOMINIC

DON, DONAL *see* DONALD

DONALD *m.* (*don'eld*)

From the Irish Domnall, meaning 'world mighty', through the Gaelic form Domhnall (*daw'nal*). The name is very common in the Highlands, and Donal is much used in Ireland, where it is interchangeable with Daniel (q.v.). The name was borne by six Scottish kings. A common short form is Don.

DONNA *f.* (*don'ę*)

This is the Italian word for 'lady'. It has been used as a Christian name in the 20th century, mainly in North America.

DONNCHADH *see* DENIS

DORA *f.* (*daw'rę*)

Originally, this name was a diminutive of Dorothy (q.v.), and also of Theodora, but it is now a name in its own right. It came into use at the beginning of the 19th century. A pet form is Dorrie, shared with other names like Doreen and Doris.

DORCAS *f.* (*daw'kęs*)

from the Greek meaning 'gazelle'. In the New Testament it was used as a Greek translation for the Aramaic Tabitha (q.v.), the name of the woman raised from the dead by St. Peter. The name was later used to describe groups of women who made clothes for the needy. Both names were popular in the

17th century among the Puritans, but are now very rare.

DORCHAIDH *see* D'ARCY

DOREEN *f.* (*daw′rēn, dawrēn′*)

from the Irish Doirean, possibly an adaptation of Dorothy (q.v.). Some sources derive it from the Celtic word for 'sullen'. It came into general use in Britain at the beginning of the 20th century with the Celtic revival, and the appearance of the name in literature inspired by the Irish revolutionary movement. The name is now very common. A short form is Dorrie.

DORINDA *f.* (*dawrin′dẹ*)

This name was invented in the 18th century as a poetic variation of Dora and Dorothy (qq.v.). Many other forms, like Belinda and Clarinda, were invented at this time.

DORIS *f.* (*dor′is*)

This is the name of a sea nymph in Greek mythology. Its meaning is unknown, though it probably has connections with the Dorian tribe. In classical literature it was a poetic name. It came into use at the end of the 19th century and is still fairly common.

DOROTHEA, DOROTHY *f.*
(*dorothē'e, do'rothi*)

from the Greek meaning 'gift of God'. The name is found in Britain from the end of the 15th century and has been in use ever since. In the 16th century it was abbreviated to Doll(y), and was so popular that the common plaything of young girls was called after it. In Scotland a doll is sometimes called a Dorrity. Shakespeare's character Doll Tearsheet, and its use in this form as a name for an immoral woman, caused it to fall into disfavour for a time. Later short forms are Dora, Dot, Dottie, Dodo and Dodie. An unusual shortened form was used by Charles Dickens for his novel *Little Dorrit*.

DORRIE *see* **DORA, DOREEN**

DORRIT, DORRITY *see* **DOROTHEA**

DOT, DOTTIE *see* **DOROTHEA**

DOUG, DOUGIE *see* **DOUGLAS**

DOUGAL, DUGALD m. (*dōō'gal*)

---

from the Irish *dubh gall*, meaning 'black stranger', a name given by the Irish to the Norwegians and still used to describe an Englishman. It is quite a common Christian name in the Highlands, and is often used as a lowland nickname for a Highlander.

DOUGLAS m. (*dug'lęs*)

---

from Gaelic *dubh glas*, meaning 'dark blue' or grey. It was first a Celtic river name, then the surname of a powerful Scottish family, famous for their strength and bravery in fighting, and from about the late 16th century, a Christian name for both girls and boys. It is still a common name for boys, especially in Scotland. Duggie, Dougie and Doug are pet forms.

DOWSABEL *see* **DULCIE**

DREW *m.* (*dróŏ*)

from the Old French meaning 'sturdy',
possibly through the Old German for
'strength' or Old German Drogo meaning 'to carry' or 'bear'. This name was
brought to Britain by the Normans.
The name also occurs in Old Welsh.
It is a fairly unusual name, but is sometimes used as an abbreviation for
Andrew (q.v.).

DROGO *see* **DREW**

DRUSILLA *f.* (*dróŏsil'ẹ*)

a feminine diminutive of the Latin
Drusus, a Roman clan name. It occurs
in the New Testament and was adopted
in the 17th century by Puritans. It is
still used occasionally, mainly in North
America.

DRYSTAN *see* **TRISTRAM**

DUDLEY *m.* (*dud'li*)

originally a surname derived from the
place of that name in Worcestershire.
The Dudley family rose to power under

the Tudors. Robert Dudley, Earl of Leicester was the favourite of Queen Elizabeth for many years. Like other aristocratic names it was adopted for general use as a Christian name in the 19th century.

DUGGIE *see* **DOUGLAS**

DUKE *see* **MARMADUKE**

DULCIBELLA *see* **DULCIE**

DULCIE *f. (dul'si)*

This name is a recent derivation of the Latin *dulcis*, meaning 'sweet' and is not from the Latin name Dulcibella, which is the source of Dowsabel, the 14th-17th century variant. Dulcibella was used in the 18th century, and Dulcie appears in the late 19th century.

DUNCAN *m. (dun'ken)*

from the Irish Donnchadh, meaning 'brown warrior'. It was the name of two Scottish kings and as a name it is almost entirely confined to Scotland. The Irish equivalent is Denis (q.v.).

DUNSTAN m. (dun'stẹn)

from the Old English compound of *dun*, meaning 'hill', and *stan*, meaning 'stone'. It was the name of a famous 10th century Archbishop of Canterbury. It appears from time to time before the Reformation, and was revived by the Oxford Movement in the 19th century.

DURAND m. (du'rẹnd)

possibly from the Latin meaning 'enduring'. It was brought to Britain by the Normans, but has never been common.

DURANTE *see* **DANTE**

DWIGHT m. (dwīt)

originally an English surname. The use of this name as a Christian name in the U.S.A. probably arose through Timothy Dwight, President of Yale, 1795-1817. The 20th century U.S. President, Dwight D. Eisenhower gave a wider circulation to the name.

DYLAN *m.* (*dilen*)

This is the name of a legendary Welsh hero, son of the sea-god, possibly meaning 'son of the wave'. It is rare outside Wales, but the Welsh poet Dylan Thomas has made the name more familiar to the general public.

DYMP(H)NA *f.* (*dimf'ne, dimp'ne*)

the anglicised form of the Irish Damhnait, the name of an Irish virgin martyr. It possibly means 'one fit to be'.

E

EACHAN *see* **HECTOR**

EADGYTH *see* **EDITH**

EALDFRITH *see* **ALFRED**

EAMON *see* **EDMOND**

EARL *m.* (*erl*)

from the Old English meaning a 'nobleman' or 'chief'. This British title has been used as a Christian name in the last hundred years, mainly in North America. Erle is a variant spelling, seen in Erle Stanley Gardner the author.

EARTHA *f.* (*er'the*)

from Old English *eorthe*, meaning 'earth'. A well-known modern example is Eartha Kitt, the singer and actress, but the name is rather uncommon.

EASTER *m. and f.* (*ēs'tẹ*)

Like the other religious festivals, this is sometimes used as a Christian name, usually for children born at that time of year. As a girl's name it is sometimes confused with Esther (q.v.).

EBEN *see* EBENEZER

EBENEZER *m.* (*ebenē'zẹ*)

from the Hebrew meaning 'stone of help'. In the Old Testament it is the name of a stone which Samuel placed between Mizpah and Shen and called Ebenezer, in memory of the triumph of the Jews over the Philistine army. It was first used as a Christian name in the 17th century among Puritans. It is now used mainly in North America, with the shortened form Eben.

ECTOR *see* **HECTOR**

ED, EDDIE *see* **EDGAR, EDMOND, EDWARD**

EDA *see* **ADA**

EDAN, EDANA *see* **EDNA**

EDEN *m.* (*ē′dẹn*)

from the Hebrew meaning 'delight'. Like other Old Testament place names it has been used as a Christian name since the 17th century, when the Puritans first adopted it, but has never been common.

EDGAR *m.* (*ed′gẹ*)

from the Old English meaning 'happy spear'. Owing to the popularity of King Edgar, King Alfred's grandson, the name continued in use after the Norman Conquest, but it faded out at the end of the 13th century. It was revived with other Old English names by 18th century writers of fiction. Its great popularity in the 19th century probably stems from its use for the hero of Scott's novel *The Bride of Lammermoor*. It is a fairly unusual name, sometimes shortened to Ed or Eddie.

EDIE *see* **EDITH**

EDINA *see* **EDNA**

EDITH *f.* (*ē′dith*)

from the Old English name Eadgyth, meaning 'prosperous war'. There were at least two English saints of that name in the 10th century. The name survived the Norman Conquest and was probably adopted by the Normans and used to transliterate several English names. Edith was in use throughout the Middle Ages, after which it became rather rare, but it returned to favour in the 19th century and is still very popular. Among the many famous 20th century holders of the name are the heroic nurse Edith Cavell, Dame Edith Sitwell the poet and Dame Edith Evans the actress. The name is often shortened to Edie.

EDMOND, EDMUND *m.* (*ed'mend*)

from the Old English Eadmund, meaning 'happy protection'. It was the name of two kings of England and of two saints. Edmond is the French form which was used in the late Middle Ages, Eamon is the Irish form. It has remained in use till the present day but is now less popular than it was in the 19th century. It has been made famous by Sir Edmund Hillary, the New Zealand mountaineer who conquered Everest. Shortened forms are Ed, Eddie and Ted.

EDNA *f.* (*ed'ne*)

The etymology of this name is obscure. It may be derived from the obsolete Old English name Edana, meaning 'happiness' or 'rich gift' Another possibility exists in a feminine form of the Celtic name Edan meaning 'fire'. It may also derive from another obsolete Old English name Edina, which is probably a feminine form of Edwin (q.v.). The name occurs several times in the

Apocrypha and its Hebrew meaning is probably 'rejuvenation'. The modern use of it may stem from the popularity of Edna Lyall's novels in the late 19th century.

EDWARD *m. (ed'wĕd)*

from the Old English meaning 'rich guardian'. Edward the Confessor established its popularity in England and ensured its survival after the Norman Conquest. It was further strengthened by the accession of Edward I, after which there was an Edward on the English throne for over a hundred years. It has remained popular in Britain ever since. The youngest of Queen Elizabeth II's four children is called Edward and this had undoubtedly made the name more popular in the 1960's. The short forms Ned and Ted have been used since the 14th century, but Ed or Eddie is more common today, together with Neddy and Teddy. The reign of Edward VII in Britain, 1901-1910, is called the Edwardian period, and more recently, young men wearing clothes which imitated the Edwardian style were called Teddy Boys.

EDWIN *m.* (*ed'win*)

from the Old English meaning 'rich friend'. It is the name of the first Christian king of Northumbria in the 7th century, who is said to have given it to the city of Edinburgh. The name survived the Norman Conquest and became popular in the 18th century. It was quite common in the 19th century, and Dickens used the name for the title of his last novel, *Edwin Drood*. It is still used occasionally. Edwina is a modern feminine form.

EDWINA *see* EDWIN

EFFIE *see* EUPHEMIA

EGBERT *m.* (*eg'bet*)

from the Old English meaning 'sword bright', the name of the first King of all England and of a 7th century Northumbrian saint who was very influential in Ireland. It enjoyed some degree of popularity in the 19th century, but is now very rarely found.

EIBHILIN *see* **EVELINE**

EILEEN, AILEEN *f.* (*ī'lēn*)

probably a development of Evelyn (q.v.). In Ireland it is often used as the equivalent of Helen. Like other Irish names it spread through out Britain at the beginning of the 20th century. Eily and Eilidh are short forms.

EILIDH, EILY *see* **EILEEN**

EITHNE *see* **AITHNE**

ELAIN *see* **ELAINE**

ELAINE *f.* (*ēlān'*)

an Old French form of Helen (q.v.) which occurs in medieval literature. It came into general use through the popularity of Tennyson's *Idylls of the King* (1859) based on Malory's *Morte D'Arthur* which include the story of *Lancelot and Elaine*. There is also a Welsh name Elain, meaning 'fawn'.

ELEANOR (A) *see* ELINOR

ELENA, ELLEN *see* HELEN

ELFREDA, ELFRIDA *f.* (*elfrē'dę*)

from the Old English compound meaning 'elfin' and 'strength'. It was the name of an Anglo-Saxon queen, wife of Edgar, and mother of Ethelred the Unready. After the Norman Conquest the name became obsolete, but it was revived in the 19th century. It is very rarely found today.

ELI *m.* (*ē'lī*)

from the Hebrew meaning 'height', and the name of the high priest in the Old Testament who looked after the prophet Samuel in the Temple. It was adopted as a Christian name in the 17th century. It is also a shortened form of Elias (q.v.), Eliza and Elihu.

ELIAS, ELIJAH *m.* (*ēlī'ęs, ēlī'ję*)

from the Hebrew meaning 'Jehovah is God'. It was very common in the

Middle Ages, with its diminutives Ellis and Eliot which became surnames. Elijah regained popularity with the Puritans in the 17th century, but neither form is much used today.

ELIHU *see* ELI

ELINOR, ELEANORE, ELEANOR(A) *f. (el'ene, elenor'e)*

These are forms of Helen (q.v.), derived from French and introduced by Eleanor of Aquitaine, who married Henry II. It was popular in the Middle Ages, and was further strengthened when Edward I erected beautiful stone crosses in memory of his wife, Eleanor of Castile, who died in 1290. It has been used ever since, often in its shortened form Nell. A famous modern holder of the name is Eleanor Roosevelt, philanthropist wife of the former U.S. President.

ELIOT *see* ELIAS

ELISABET, ELIZABETHA *see* ELIZABETH

ELISHA *m. (eli'she)*

from the Hebrew meaning 'God is salvation'. This Biblical name was used mostly by Puritans in the 17th century in Britain, and is still current in North America.

ELISHEBA *see* **ELIZABETH**

ELIZA *see* **ELI, ELIZABETH**

ELIZABETH, ELISABETH *f.*
(eliz'ebeth)

from the Hebrew Elisheba, meaning 'oath of God' or 'God has sworn'. The present form developed from the Greek Elisabet through the Latin Elizabetha to Elizabeth. In Britain the 'z' form is usual, on the Continent the 's' is used. It was first used as a Christian name in the Eastern Church, and found its way across Europe to France, where it had the form Isabel (q.v.). This was also the usual medieval form in England. Elizabeth became common about the end of the 15th century, and its later popularity in England stemmed from the long reign of Elizabeth I. Among the many diminutives the following have been most used: Bess(ie), Betsy, Betty, Beth, Eliza, Lizzy, Liz, Libby and the Scottish Elspeth, Elspie and Elsie (see ELSA), which are now used independently. The German Elsa (q.v.), Lisa, Liesel, the Italian Bettina, and the French Elise, Lisette and Babette, are also used in Britain.

ELLA *f.* (*el'e̞*)

a name used by the Normans, but probably derived from the Old German Alia, a feminine name from *alja*, meaning 'all'. It may also be a variant of Ellen (q.v.). It was revived in the 19th century and is now fairly common. A well-known modern example is Ella Fitzgerald the jazz singer.

ELLEN *f.* (*el'e̞n*)

This is an older English form of Helen (q.v.), now used independently. It is especially popular in Scotland and Ireland.

ELLIS *see* **ELIAS**

ELMA *f.* (*el'mĕ*)

The origin of this name is obscure, but it is thought to be a combination of the beginning of Elizabeth and Mary.

ELMER *m.* (*el'mĕ*)

This name is derived either from Aylmer (q.v.), or Old English Ethelmer, and means 'noble'. Its use in the U.S.A. probably stems from two brothers with the surname Elmer, who were prominent in the American War of Independence.

ELSA, ELSIE *f.* (*el'sĕ, el'si*)

The probable source for Elsa is the Old German meaning 'noble one'. However, both names are used as abbreviations of Elizabeth, and Elsie is sometimes the short form of Alison. Elsie is predominantly Scottish, and the more common form in Britain. Elsa is the heroine of Richard Wagner's opera *Lohengrin* and this made the name popular in the 19th century.

ELSIE *see* **ELIZABETH**

ELSPETH, ELSPIE *see* **ELIZABETH**

ELUNED *f.* (*eli'ned*)

This is a Welsh name, the origin of which is obscure. It is seldom used outside Wales.

ELVIRA *f.* (*elvēr'ę*)

a Spanish name, possibly derived from an Old German word meaning 'elf counsel'. It has been used occasionally since the beginning of the 19th century.

EMANUEL *m.* (*ēman'ūel*)

from the Hebrew meaning 'God with us'. It was the name given to the promised Messiah by the prophet Isaiah in the Old Testament. It was first used as a Christian name by the Greeks in the form Manuel. This is also the Spanish form. Both Emanuel and Manuel are found in Cornwall in the 15th and 16th centuries, but they never became common. The name was very popular among Jews, who also used the shortened form Manny. But this use seems to be declining.

EMELYE see EMILY

EMILY, EMILIA f. (em'ili, emē'lie)

from Latin Aemilius, the name of a Roman plebeian clan. Boccaccio, the 14th century Italian writer, used Emilia, popularising this form in the Middle Ages, and Chaucer borrowed it in the form Emelye. The name has persisted since then, becoming very common as Emily in the 19th century, when it was sometimes shortened to Emma (q.v.). Milly is another short form.

EMLYN m. (em'lin)

a common Welsh name, possibly derived from Latin Aemilianus or a variant of Ermin. It is also found as an English feminine name derived from the Old German meaning 'serpent of work'.

EM(M) see EMMA

EMMA *f.* (*em'ę*)

from a shortened form of an Old German compound of *ermin*, meaning 'universal'. It was introduced into England by Emma, daughter of Richard I, Duke of Normandy. The 11th century Queen Emma was a very popular figure called 'the fair maid of Normandy'. The English form was Em(m), and this was used until the mid 18th century, when the original form was revived. At this time Jane Austen wrote her novel *Emma*. Today Emma is one of the commonest girl's names. A derivative is Ermyntrude (q.v.).

EMMELINE *f.* (*em'elēn*)

from the Old French diminutives of Emilia and Emily (q.v.). The Normans introduced the name to England in the 11th century, in many variant forms like Emblem and Emblin, but Emmeline is the one most often found.

ENA *f.* (*ē'nę*)

an anglicised form of the Irish Aithne

(q.v.). Its popularity in England is probably partly due to Princess Ena, who was born in 1887, and who became Queen of Spain. It is also possibly derived from the Greek word meaning 'praise', as the feminine form of Aeneas (q.v.).

ENID *f.* (*ē'nid, en'id*)

This is a Welsh name that came into use in England in the 19th century, through Tennyson's poem *Geraint and Enid* in the *Idylls of the King* (1859). Its meaning is uncertain but it has been connected with the Welsh *enit*, meaning 'wood-bark'.

ENOCH *m.* (*ē'nok*)

from the Hebrew meaning 'trained', 'skilled' or 'dedicated'. It was the name of an Old Testament patriarch and was adopted in the 17th century by the Puritans. Tennyson's *Enoch Arden* (1864) may have helped to preserve it, but it is now rare. A well-known modern example is Enoch Powell, the politician.

EOGHAN *see* EVAN

EPHRAIM *m.* (ĕ′frām, ĕ′frĕm)

from the Hebrew meaning 'fruitful', an Old Testament name that was revived in the 17th century by the Puritans. It is seldom used in England, but is still found in North America.

EPPIE *see* EUPHEMIA

ERASMUS *m.* (eraz′mĕs)

from the Greek meaning 'beloved', and the name of an early Christian martyr. The Dutch scholar and religious reformer Desiderius Erasmus (1465-1536) made the name famous, although it was used in Britain before his influence was exerted.

ERASTUS *m.* (erast′ĕs)

from the Greek meaning 'beloved'. The short form Rastus is better known in Britain and in North America, but the name is rare.

ERIC m. (e'rik)

from Norse; the second syllable means 'ruler'; the first is doubtful, but possibly means 'ever'. The name was brought to Britain about the 9th century by the Danes and its use has been spasmodic ever since. Possibly Dean Farrar's book *Eric or Little by Little* was largely responsible for its revival in the 19th century. It is now very popular. Erica is the feminine form, now sometimes identified with the Latin botanical name for heather. Short forms are Rex and Rickie or Rick, and in North America, Air and Erie.

ERICA see ERIC

ERIE see ERIC

ERMIN see EMLYN

ERMYNTRUDE f. (e'mintrŏŏd)

from the Old German meaning 'universal strength'. It was adopted by 18th and 19th century romantic writers and as a result it was occasionally used as a Christian name. It is now obsolete.

ERN, ERNIE *see* **ERNEST**

ERNEST, EARNEST *m.* (*er'nist*)

from the Old German meaning 'vigour' or 'earnestness'. It was introduced by the Hanoverians in the late 18th century and was common in the 19th century. Oscar Wilde's play, *The Importance of Being Earnest* (1899), increased its popularity. Ernestine is the feminine form but, like Ernest, it is not very common today. Shortened forms are Ern and Ernie. The latter is the acronym nickname commonly used in Britain for Electronic Random Number Indicating Equipment, the premium bond prize selector.

ERNESTINE *see* **ERNEST**

ERROL *m.* (*er'el*)

It is not certain whether this name is a development of Eral, a medieval form of Harold (q.v.), or whether it is a variant of Earl (q.v.). Errol Flynn, the film actor, was a well-known recent example. It may also be connected with the Irish word for 'pledge'.

ESMÉ *m. and f. (ez′mā)*

probably synonymous with the French Aimé, meaning 'beloved'. It passed from France to Scotland and the Stuart family in the 16th century, and then to England, but not until much later. It is now more often used as a girl's name.

ESMERALDA(H) *f. (ezmeral′de)*

Spanish for 'emerald'. It was used by the French 19th century writer Victor Hugo for the heroine in his novel *The Hunchback of Notre Dame*, and it has occasionally been used since in Britain and France.

ESMOND *m. (ez′mend)*

from the Old English compound of 'grace' or 'beauty' and 'protection'. The name was never common, and fell out of use in the 14th century. Its modern use dates from Thackeray's novel *The History of Henry Esmond* (1852). It is nowadays rather rare.

ESS, ESSIE, ESSY *see* ESTHER

ESTELLE *f.* (*estel'*)

from the latin *stella* and the French *étoile* meaning 'star'. It was a French name given by the 19th century novelist, Dickens, to the heroine of *Great Expectations*, and it has been used quite frequently since. It sometimes shares the shortened forms of Esther (q.v.).

ESTHER *f.* (*es'te̞*)

in the Old Testament the name is given as the Persian equivalent of a Hebrew word meaning 'myrtle'. It was interchangeable with Hester and appears in England in the 17th century, adopted by the Puritans. Racine's play *Esther* helped to popularise it in the 17th century, especially in France. It is not very common today. Shortened forms include Essy, Essie and Ess.

ETHEL *f.* (*eth'e̞l*)

This name was not originally independent. It arose in the 19th century as a shortening of various Anglo-Saxon names beginning with the root Ethel-, from the Old English *aethel*, meaning 'noble'. Its vogue in the 19th century was due to its use by popular authors like Thackeray. It has fallen out of favour in the 20th century.

ETHELBERT *m.* (*eth'elbet*)

from the Old English meaning 'noble bright', and the name of a 6th century Anglo-Saxon king. A convert to Christianity and the teachings of St. Augustine, he was the first Archbishop of Canterbury. The name died out after the Norman Conquest, having only a brief revival in the 19th century.

ETHELMER *see* ELMER

ETHELRED *m.* (*e'thelred*)

from the Old English meaning 'noble counsel', a fairly common Old English name. It probably died out after the Norman Conquest but was revived in the 19th century during a period in which Old English names were favoured.

ETHELREDA *see* **AUDREY**

ETHNE, EITHNE *see* **AITHNE**

ETTA *see* **ADA, HENRIETTA**

EUFEMIA *see* **EUPHEMIA**

EUGENE *m.* (*ūzhēn'*)

from the Greek meaning 'well-born', and the name of four popes. Its use in Britain and France was largely due to the fame of the 18th century Prince Eugène of Savoy, the great general and ally of Marlborough. In North America it is usually abbreviated to Gene. Eugenia and Eugénie (*uzhē'nię, uzhā'ni*) are feminine forms.

EUGENIA, EUGÉNIE *see* **EUGENE**

EUGENIUS *see* **OWEN**

EULALIA *f.* (*ūlā'lię*)

from the Greek meaning 'sweetly speaking', and the name of a 4th century martyr of Barcelona. It is popular in Spain and France, and has been used occasionally in Britain.

EUNICE *f.* (*ūni′s*)

from the Greek meaning 'happy victory' or possibly 'wife'. The name is mentioned in the New Testament and was adopted by Puritans in the 17th century. It is still used today but not widely.

EUPHEME *see* **EUPHEMIA**

EUPHEMIA *f.* (*ūfě′mię*)

from the Greek meaning 'fair speech', or by implication, 'silence'. It occurs as Eufemia and Eupheme from the 12th century. Later it became confined to Scotland, where it is still found, often abbreviated to Effie or Eppie.

EUSTACE *m.* (*ū′stęs*)

from the Greek meaning 'rich in corn' and hence 'fruitful' generally. Because of the two saints Eustachius this name was in use in Britain before the Norman Conquest, and was popular from the 12th to the 16th century. The Italian Renaissance physician Eustachio gave his name to the Eustachian tubes connecting the ear and throat. There is a rare feminine form Eustacia which was also used in the 18th and 19th centuries.

EUSTACHIO *see* EUSTACE

EUSTACHIUS *see* EUSTACE

EUSTACIA *see* EUSTACE

EVADNE *f.* (*evad'ni*)

This is Greek name of uncertain meaning. It was used occasionally in the early part of the 20th century.

EVAN *m.* (*ev'ẹn*)

This is a the Welsh form of John (q.v.). It is also an anglicised form of the Irish Eoghan, which became Evan and Ewan in Scotland. It dates from about 1500 and is still common in Wales.

EVANGELINE *f.* (*ivan'jẹlēn*)

from the Greek meaning 'evangel', 'bringer of good tidings', and first introduced by Longfellow for his poem *Evangeline* (1847). It is used fairly often in North America and occasionally in Britain.

EVE, EVA *f.* (*ēv′, ē′vē*)

from the Hebrew meaning 'life', and in the Old Testament, the name of the first woman. Eva is the Latin form, Eve the vernacular. It was in use in Britain even before the Reformation, when Old Testament names were not generally popular. In Ireland it was probably substituted for the earlier Gaelic Aoiffe, meaning 'pleasant'. It is still a common name in both forms. The pet form is Evie.

EVELINE, EVELINA *f.* (*evelēn, evelēne*)

There are two possible sources for this name. It may derive from the Irish meaning 'pleasant', the commonest form of the name in Ireland being Eveleen, or from the Old German variant of the name Avi, which was brought to England by the Normans, and was the basis of many surnames like Evelyn and Eveling. The surname Evelyn was almost certainly the major source of the use of Evelyn as a masculine, and later feminine, Christian name. It is often used to transliterate the Gaelic Eibhilin, meaning 'light'.

EVELYN *f.* (*ēv'elin, ev'elin*)

This name is probably derived partly from the same source as Eveline (q.v.), and partly through the former popularity of the name in its masculine use. This girl's name is now quite common.

EVELYN *m.* (*ēv'lin*)

This name was used as a masculine personal name in Britain around the 17th century, and was derived from the surname. Its popularity has now declined and this may have something to do with the much more common use of the feminine Evelyn (q.v.).

EVERARD *m.* (*ev'eràd*)

from the Old German for 'boar' and 'hard'. This French form was brought to Britain by the Normans and was fairly common in England in the 12th and 13th centuries. It has been used occasionally since.

EVERILO *see* **AVERIL**

EVIE *see* **EVE**

EWAN, EWEN *m.* (*ū'ẹn*)

from the Irish Eoghan meaning 'a youth'. Though once common in England, it is now mostly confined to Scotland. It is probably equivalent to the Welsh Owen (q.v.).

EZEKIEL *m.* (*ezē'kiẹl*)

from the Hebrew meaning 'may God strengthen'. It is the name of an Old Testament prophet, and was used from the 17th century in Britain. It is still current in North America, where Zeke is the usual abbreviation.

EZRA *m.* (*ez'rẹ*)

from the Hebrew meaning 'help', the name of the author of one of the Old Testament books. It was adopted as a Christian name by Puritans in the 17th century. The name is no longer common. A well-known example in the 20th century is Ezra Pound the American poet.

F

FABIAN m. (*fā'biən*)

from the Latin family name Fabianus, possibly meaning 'bean-grower'. There was a pope and a Saint Fabian in the 3rd century, and there is a record of the name being used by a sub-prior of St. Albans in the 13th century. There is little other evidence of it until the 16th century, but its use as a surname shows that it was known previously. It has not been widely used since then. The Roman general Fabius, known as the 'delayer' for his tactics, was the inspiration for the Fabian Society, a socialist society founded in 1884.

FABIUS *see* FABIAN

FAGAN, FAGIN *m.* (*fā′gen, fā′gin*)

from Irish Gaelic meaning 'little fiery one'. This predominantly Irish name is perhaps best known for Charles Dickens' character, Fagin, in *Oliver Twist.*

FAITH *f.* and *m.* (*fāth*)

one of the Christian virtues used as names after the Reformation. It was formerly used for both sexes, but is now more common as a girl's name.

FANNY *see* **FRANCES**

FARQUHAR *m.* (*fà′ke*)

from the Gaelic words meaning 'man' and 'friendly'. It was the name of one of the kings of Scotland and is still often used in the Highlands.

FARRAND, FARRANT, FARREN *see* **FERDINAND**

FAY *f.* (*fā*)

from French, probably meaning 'fairy'. It is also possible that it is an abbreviation of Faith (q.v.).

FELICE, FELIS *see* **FELIX**

FELICIA *see* **FELIX**

FELICITAS *see* **FELICITY**

FELICITY *f.* (*felis'iti*)

from the Latin meaning 'happiness', and, in the form Felicitas, the name of two saints. It was used by the Puritans in the 17th century, and it is fairly common today.

FELIX *m.* (*fe'lix*)

from the Latin meaning 'happy', the name of many saints and four popes. It was widely used in the Middle Ages, and had a fairly strong hold in Ireland, where it transliterated the Irish Phelim. The feminine form Felicia has a long history of use, and was also very popular in the Middle Ages. Variant forms were Felice and Felis.

FENELLA *f.* (*fenel'e*)

from the Irish words meaning 'white' and 'shoulder'. The name became known in Britain in the 19th century as a result

of Scott's novel *Peveril of the Peak*, but
it has never been common. A derivative
is Finola.

FERDINAND *m.* (*fer′dinend*)

from the Old German words meaning
'journey' and 'venture'. The name was
never popular in Germany but was
common in Spain, especially in the
forms Fernando and Hernando, and in
Italy as Ferrante and Ferdinando. It
was fairly popular in England and
France in the form Ferrand, which was
the origin of the surnames Farrand,
Farrant and Farren. The Italian form
Ferdinando was used in England in the
16th and 17th centuries, especially
among the gentry in the Midlands. It
is not uncommon today.

FERDINANDO *see* FERDINAND

FERGUS, FEARGUS *m.* (*fer′ges*)

from the Irish words for 'man' and
'choice', and a fairly common Christian name in Scotland and Ireland. It
is also used in the North of England.

FERNANDO *see* **FERDINAND**

FERRAND *see* **FERDINAND**

FERRANTE *see* **FERDINAND**

FINOLA *see* **FENELLA**

FIONA *f.* (*fēŏ'nĕ*)

---

from the Gaelic meaning 'fair'. It was used in the 19th century by William Sharp as a pen name (Fiona Macleod). It is now a popular Christian name, especially in Scotland.

FLEUR *f.* (*flĕr*)

---

from the French meaning 'flower'. It was first used as a Christian name in the 20th century, in Galsworthy's book *The Forsyte Saga*. It is occasionally used in Britain. The English form Flower is also found.

FLO, FLOY *see* **FLORENCE**

FLORA *f.* (*flaw'rĕ*)

---

from the Latin meaning 'flower'. Flora was the Roman goddess of flowers and the spring. It is now a fairly popular

Christian name in Britain, especially in the Highlands. A famous holder of the name was Flora Macdonald, who played an important part in the escape of Bonnie Prince Charlie after Culloden in 1746. Well known in the 20th century is the actress, Dame Flora Robson.

FLORENCE f. (flor'ens)

from the Latin name Florentius, used by the Romans for both males and females, and derived from the word meaning 'blooming'. In the Middle Ages, Florence was used as often for a man as for a woman, but it has since ceased to be used as a man's name. Florence Nightingale was named after the town in Italy, and her fame popularised the name in the 19th century. It is still fairly common. Abbreviated forms are Florrie, Flossie, Floy and Flo.

FLORRIE, FLOSSIE
see **FLORENCE**

FLOWER *see* **FLEUR**

FLOYD *see* **LLOYD**

FRANCES *f.* (*fràn'sis*)

from the feminine form of the Italian
Francesco (*see* FRANCIS). Francesca was
first used in Italy in the 13th century,
and, at about the same time, Françoise
began to appear in France. The name
was not used in Britain until the 15th
century, and it became popular with the
English aristocracy at the time of the
Tudors. It is now generally used throughout Britain, the short form being Fanny.
Other diminutive forms are Francie and
Frankie.

FRANCESCA, FRANCESCO
see **FRANCES**

FRANCIE, FRANKIE *see* **FRANCIS, FRANCES**

FRANCIS *m.* (*fràn'sis*)

from the Latin meaning 'Frenchman'.
The name became popular in Europe
in the 15th century because of St.
Francis of Assisi. The Italian word
Francesco was in fact only the Saint's
nickname, his Christian name being

Giovanni. It was first used in Britain in the 15th century, and the fame of Francis Drake, a century later, made the name better known. It has become very popular in Britain today. Frank is an abbreviation which is now given as a separate name.

FRANÇOISE *see* **FRANCES**

FRANK *see* **FRANCIS**

FRANKLIN *m.* (*frank'lin*)

from Middle English. In medieval times a franklin was a man who had earned his freedom from his feudal overlord, and owned land in his own right. A famous modern example was Franklin D. Roosevelt, the 32nd U.S. President.

FRED, FREDDIE, FREDDY *see* **ALFRED, FREDERICK**

FREDA *see* **WINIFRED**

FREDERICA, FREDERIKA *see* **FREDERICK**

FREDERICK *m. (fred'rik)*

from the Old German meaning 'peaceful ruler'. The German form Friedrich was the name of several emperors and of King Frederick the Great of Prussia. It is very popular today and common abbreviations are Fred, Freddie and Freddy. The feminine form is Frederica (ka). It is unusual in Britain but currently known through Queen Frederika of Greece .

FRIEDRICH *see* FREDERICK

G

GABRIEL *m. (gā'briel)*

from Hebrew, containing the elements 'God', 'man' and 'strength', and possibly implying the phrase 'strong man of God'. In St. Luke's gospel it is the name of the archangel of the Annunciation. The name has been used infrequently since the Middle Ages. Gabrielle is the feminine form, taken from the French masculine name.

GABRIELLE *see* **GABRIEL**

GAIL *see* **ABIGAIL**

GARETH *m.* (*gar'eth*)

from the Welsh meaning 'gentle'. This name was used by the 16th century writer Malory in his *Morte d'Arthur*, and later by Tennyson, the 19th century poet, in *Gareth and Lynnette*. It was due to the latter that the name was revived in this century, but it has never become common. Garth and Gar(r)y are modern contractions.

GARFIELD *m.* (*gä'feld*)

a rare name, derived from the Old English meaning 'spear field'.

GARNIER *see* **WARNER**

GARRETT *see* **GERARD**

GARRY *see* **GARETH**

GARTH *see* **GARETH**

GASPAR, GASPARD *see* **JASPER**

GASTON m. (gas'tong)

from French. The name was originally
spelt Gascon and meant a man from
Gascony. Today it is a common French
Christian name, and it has been used
occasionally in Britain also.

GAVIN see GAWAIN

GAWAIN m. (gà'wān)

from the Welsh meaning 'hawk of May'.
It was the name of King Arthur's
nephew in Welsh legend. Sir Gawain
became one of the best known characters
of Arthurian romance. He is sometimes
referred to as Walwain, which suggests
a link with Old English Walwyn,
'friend in battle'. There is also an Old
German name Gawin, derived from a
word meaning 'a district of land'.
Gavin is a French form which came
to Britain in the Middle Ages and is
still found today, especially in Scotland.

GAWIN see GAWAIN

GAY *f.* (*gā*)

This name is simply the adjective meaning happy and lively, and its use is very recent. It is a common name in Britain and in North America, where it probably first arose.

GEMMA *f.* (*jem'ẹ*)

This is the Italian for 'gem', and there is one isolated example of this name's use in the 13th century. It has been used very occasionally in Britain since then.

GENE *see* **EUGENE**

GENEVIEVE *f.* (*jen'ẹvēv*)

a French name from an Old German compound name meaning 'woman of the race'. It is found in Latin records as Genovera and Genoveva. St. Geneviève is the patron saint of Paris; she saved the city from the Huns in the 15th century by her cool thinking and courage, and the name is very popular in France. It has been used in Britain since the 19th century.

GENOVERA, GENOVEVA
see **GENEVIEVE**

GEOFF *see* **GEOFFREY**

GEOFFREY, JEFFREY *m.* (*jef'ri*)

from the Old German Gaufrid, meaning
'district peace'. The name seems also
to have assimilated the Old German
Gisfrid, meaning 'pledge peace'. Geoffrey
was popular between the 12th and 15th
centuries in England, resulting in many
surnames e.g. Jeffries, Jeeves, Jepson.
Two famous medieval Geoffreys were
Chaucer, the father of English literature,
and Geoffrey of Monmouth, the 12th
century historian. It fell from favour from
the 15th to the 19th century, when it
returned to fashion. Geoff and Jeff are
common abbreviations.

GEORDIE *see* **GEORGE**

GEORGE *m.* (*jawj'*)

from the Greek meaning 'tiller of the
soil' or 'farmer'. The famous St. George
may have been a Roman soldier who

was martyred in Palestine in A.D. 303.
In early Christian art many saints were
represented as trampling on a dragon, as
a symbol of good conquering evil. This
may be the explanation of how the legend
of St. George and the dragon originated.
He was described as the personification
of chivalry in medieval writing. From
1349, when Edward III founded the
Order of the Garter and put it under
St. George's patronage, the latter was
regarded as the patron saint of England.
Despite this, the name was never much
used until the Hanoverian succession
in 1714 brought a line of Georges to
the throne. Geordie is a Scottish and
North Country pet form which is used
as a nick-name for Northumbrians in
general.

GEORGES *see* GEORGE

GEORGINA *f.* (*jawjĕn'ę*)

This is the most common feminine form
of George (q.v.). It was first used in
Britain in the 18th century, when
George became popular. The form then

was Georgiana, which is still sometimes used. Other feminine forms of George are Georgia, Georgette and Georgine.

GER, GERRY *see* GERALD

GERAINT *m.* (*gerīnt', jerānt'*)

This is a Welsh name, a variant form of the Latin Gerontius, which is derived from the Greek word meaning 'old'. The 19th century poet Tennyson used the old Welsh story of *Geraint and Enid* in his *Idylls of the King,* and it was from this that the name's modern use has stemmed. Geraint Evans is a very well-known modern operatic singer.

GERALD *m.* (*jer'eld*)

from the Old German meaning 'spear rule'. It was used in England from the 11th to the 12th century and was probably introduced by the Normans. The name flourished in Ireland due to the influence of the Fitzgerald family, the powerful rulers of Kildare. It was probably from Ireland that the name returned to England in the late 19th century. It is now quite common and in Wales has the form Gerallt. Shortened forms are Ger and Gerry.

GERALDINE *f.* (*jer'eldēn*)

There is no evidence of how this name arose, other than in the works of a 16th century poet, praising the beauty of Lady Elizabeth Fitzgerald. Geraldine therefore means 'one of the Fitzgeralds'. It was very popular in the 19th century and is still fairly common.

GERALT *see* GERALD

GERARD *m.* (*jer'ard*)

from the Old German meaning 'spear hard'. It was brought to Britain by Norman settlers and was very common in the Middle Ages. The surnames Gerrard and Garrett are derived from it, and these were the most common medieval pronunciations of the Christian name. Garret is still used in Ireland, but Gerard is now fairly unusual.

GERDA f. (ger'de)

Originally appearing in Norse mythology, this Scandinavian name has been used occasionally in Britain. It was probably introduced into the country by the little girl in *The Snow Queen*, one of the popular children's stories of Hans Christian Andersen.

GERONIMUS see **JEROME**

GERONTIUS see **GERAINT**

GERT, GERTIE see **GERTRUDE**

GERTRUDE f. (ger'trŏŏd)

from the Old German meaning 'spear strength'. In Norse mythology it was the name of one of the Valkyries, or Rhine Maidens, the goddesses who transported those killed in battle to Valhalla, the palace of bliss. The name came to Britain from the Netherlands, where a saint of that name was much venerated. It appears in many forms from the Middle Ages until the 19th century, when it was finalised as Gertrude, and became very popular. It is still in use, with the pet forms Gert or Gertie and Trudie.

GERVAIS *see* GERVASE

GERVASE *m.* (*jer′vāz*)

from the Old German meaning 'spear vassal' or 'armour bearer'. The name was first used among English churchmen of the 12th century in honour of the 1st century martyr St. Gervase. It spread to the laity, giving rise to the surname Jarvis, which is still common, whereas the original has practically died out. Gervais is an alternative spelling.

GIB *see* GILBERT

GIDEON *m.* (*gid′iẹn*)

from Hebrew, now generally thought to mean 'having a stump for a hand', although the traditional translation was 'a hewer'. In the Old Testament it is the name of the Israelite leader who routed the Midianites with three hundred men. The name was adopted at the Reformation and was a favourite

among the Puritans, who took it to
North America, where it is still in use.

GILBERT *m.* (*gil'bet*)

from the Old German meaning 'pledge
bright'. The Normans brought the name
to England and it was common in
medieval times. Gilbert of the White
Hand was one of Robin Hood's companions. The name was popular in the
19th century. Two famous holders
were Gilbert White, who wrote the
Natural History of Selborne, and the
librettist half of the famous 'Gilbert
and Sullivan' partnership of light opera
composers. The latter use of Gilbert as a
surname is an example of many similar
uses in variants like Gibbs, Gibson and
Gibbons. The broadcaster Gilbert Hard-
ing made the name well-known in the
20th century. Shortened forms are Gib,
Bert and Bertie.

GILES *m.* (*jīls*)

St. Giles was an Athenian who took

his name, Aegidius, from the goatskin
that he wore. He left Greece in order
to escape the fame of his miracles, and
became a hermit in France. There the
name took root as Giles, which possibly
derived from Celtic *gille*, or 'servant,'
because of his humility, rather than a
derivative of Aegidius. The name is first
recorded in England in the 12th century, but, despite the large number of
churches dedicated to this saint, the
name was never popular. It has been
suggested that this may be because of
St. Giles' association with beggars and
cripples of whom he is the patron saint.
The name Gillies, from Gaelic *gille losa*,
meaning, 'servant of Jesus', is found both
as a surname and a Christian name in
Scotland.

GILL, GILLOT *see* **GILLIAN** (*f.*)

GILLEAN, GILLEON *see* **GILLIAN** (*m.*)

GILLES *see* **GILES**

GILLIAN *f.* (*jil'i̯ẹn, gil'i̯ẹn*)

This name, which is an English rendering of the Latin Julian (q.v.) was so common in the Middle Ages that it was used as a general term for a girl, (cf. Jack for a man). The pet forms Gill, Gillot and Gillet were common and from the last of these came the expression 'to jilt', which was why the name lost favour in the late 17th century. It was revived in the 20th century, and once more became very popular. A variant form is Jillian, and Jill, the abbreviated form, is now given as an independent name.

GILLIAN *m.* (*gil'iẹn*)

Also spelt Gillean and Gilleon, this name is probably derived from the Gaelic Gill' Eoin, meaning servant of St. John, and is found occasionally in the Highlands.

GILLIES *see* GILES

GINNY *see* VIRGINIA

GISELLE *f.* (*jizel'*)

from the Old German meaning a 'pledge'

or 'hostage'. Gisèle has for a long time been a common French name, and the English form Giselle and the latinised Gisela have been used in Britain, mainly by Roman Catholics.

GISFRID *see* **GEOFFREY**

GIULIA *see* **JULIA**

GIULIETTA *see* **JULIET**

GLAD *see* **GLADYS**

GLADYS *f.* (*glad'is*)

This is the anglicised form of Gwladys, which is generally thought to be the Welsh equivalent of Claudia (q.v.). It may have had an earlier source, but this is now lost. It was first used in England in the late 19th century, since when it has become widespread. In recent decades it has become less fashionable. It is often shortened to Glad.

GLORIA *f.* (*glaw'ri̠e*)

This is Latin for 'glory' or 'fame', and the name seems to have been coined by Bernard Shaw in 1889 in his play *You Never Can Tell*. It was very common in the first half of the 20th century, although its popularity is now waning.

GODFREY m. (god'fri)

from the Old German meaning 'God's peace'. There was an equivalent Old English name Godfrith, but the medieval Godfrey probably derives from the Norman form. It has survived until the present day and is probably as common as it has ever been.

GODFRITH see GODFREY

GORDON m. (gaw'dẹn)

This was originally a Scottish place name, probably in Berwickshire from which the local lords took their name, founding a large and famous clan. It was rarely used as a Christian name until 1885, when the tragic death of General Gordon at Khartoum gave the name immense popularity.

GRACE *f.* (*grās*)

from Latin *gratia*, meaning 'grace', in its original religious sense. This name existed as Gracia in the Middle Ages but did not become common until the Puritans adopted it, along with the names of other Christian qualities. Its popularity waned in the 18th century, but it came back into favour when Grace Darling captured the hearts of the people with her heroic exploit in 1838. With her father, the lighthouse-keeper of the Farne Islands, she rescued nine survivors from a shipwreck in a terrifying storm. Gracie, though really a pet form, is sometimes given as a separate name. The singer and comedienne Gracie Fields has made the name famous in Britain in the 20th century.

GRACIE *see* GRACE

GRAHAM *m.* (*grā'ęm*)

Like Gordon this was originally a Scottish place name which developed into a family name and gradually came into general use as a Christian name. It is now used without reference to its Scottish connections. Famous bearers of it in modern times are Graham Green, the author, and Graham Hill, a popular figure in motor racing.

GREG, GREGOR, GREGOUR
see GREGORY

GREGORY *m.* (*greg'eri*)

from the Greek meaning 'watchman'. The name first came to Britain through St. Gregory the Great, the Pope who sent St. Augustine to England. It was in common use from the time of the Norman Conquest, when most Latin names were introduced, until the Reformation when, because of its association with the Papacy, it fell out of use. Gregour was the usual medieval form, which is still found as Gregor in Scotland, and hence the surname MacGregor. The popularity of the film actor, Gregory Peck has given the name some vogue in recent years. The most common shortened form is Greg.

GRETA *f.* (*grē′tẹ*)

a Swedish abbreviation of Margaret
(q.v.). It was rare in England until the
20th century, when the fame of the film
actress Greta Garbo gave the name some
vogue.

GRETEL, GRETCHEN *f.* (*gret′ẹl,
grech′ẹn*)

The German diminutive form of Margaret (q.v.), from the Latin meaning
'pearl'. These names are rarely used
in Britain.

GRIFFITH *m.* (*grif′ith*)

from the Welsh name Gruffud, *udd*
meaning 'lord'. It has always been
fairly popular in Wales, and was the
name of several Welsh princes. It is
not, however, widely used throughout
Britain.

GRISELDA, GRIZEL *f.* (*grizel′dẹ,
griz′ẹl*)

from Old German, the meaning being
disputed but possibly 'grey battle-mai-

den'. Chaucer gave rise to its use in Britain by including it in his *Clerk's Tale*, the story of which he took from Boccaccio. The name now occurs mostly in Scotland, but it has never been popular.

GRUFFUD *see* GRIFFITH

GUARIN *see* WARREN

GUIDO *see* GUY

GUS, GUSSIE *see* AUGUSTUS

GUY *m.* (gī)

from the Old German Wido, the derivation of which is uncertain. Wido became Guido in Latin records and Guy was the French form introduced to Britain by the Normans. Apparently the medieval clergy identified the name with the Latin Vitus meaning 'lively', hence the disease St. Vitus' Dance is known in France as *la danse de Saint Guy*. St. Vitus was a Sicilian martyr who was invoked for the cure of nervous ailments. The name fell out of use after Guy Fawkes' gunpowder plot in the 17th century. It was revived in the 19th century with the help of Walter Scott's novel *Guy Mannering*. It is still a popular name in Britain.

GWEN(DA) *f.* (*gwen, gwen′dę*)

from the pet forms of several names which come from the Welsh word meaning 'white'. Gwen and Gwenda are now used as separate names, and are fairly common in Britain.

GWENDOLYN, GWENDOLEN GUENDOLEN *f.* (*gwen′dolin*)

from the Welsh meaning 'white circle', probably a reference to the ancient moon-goddess. The name occurs frequently in Welsh legend. Guendolen was the name of a fairy with whom King Arthur fell in love, and also of the wife of Merlin the magician. Gwen and Gwenda, the abbreviated forms, are today more popular than the original, and are used frequently throughout Britain.

GWLADYS *see* **GLADYS**

GWYN *m.* (*gwin*)

from the Welsh meaning 'white' or
'blessed'. This name has been anglicised
as Wyn or Wynne. It is most popular
in Wales.

GWYNETH *f.* (*gwin'eth*)

from Welsh meaning 'blessed' or 'happy'.
It is quite a common name in Wales,
and has occasionally been used in
England. Gwyn is the pet form.

H

HADRIANUS *see* **ADRIAN**

HALBERT *see* **ALBERT**

HALLAM *m.* (*hal'em*)

This is a surname which has been used
as a Christian name since 1850, when
Tennyson wrote his great elegy *In
Memoriam* about his gifted friend Arthur
Henry Hallam, who had died in 1843

aged only twenty-two. It is not a very
common name.

HAM *see* **ABRAHAM**

HAMELIN, HAMELOT, HAMONET
see **HAMO**

HAMISH *m.* (*hā′mish*)
___
the anglicised form of the Gaelic Seumas,
equivalent to James (q.v.). This name
became popular in the second half of
the 19th century, and is still common
in Scotland.

HAMO *m.* (*hā′mō*)
___
from the Old German meaning 'house'.
It became popular in England after the
Norman Conquest, with the alternative
form Hamon. Both forms are still
used very occasionally but are mainly
confined to certain families. Diminutives
include Hamelin, Hamonet and Hamelot.

HAMON *see* **HAMO**

HANNAH f. (han'ę)

from the Hebrew meaning 'He has favoured me'. In the Old Testament it was the name of Samuel's mother. It was the Greek form Anna (q.v.) which first became established throughout Europe. Hannah was only adopted in England after the Reformation. It was very common in the 17th century, but is used only occasionally in the British Isles, being confined mostly to Ireland.

HARIVIG *see* **HARVEY**

HAROLD m. (har'ęld)

from the Old Norse meaning 'army-power'. It was used in the Middle Ages, but went out of fashion until the 18th century when it became popular again. Its modern popularity stems from 19th century literature celebrating King Harold II, the last of the Saxon Kings, who fought William the Conqueror, and was killed at Hastings in 1066. It shares the abbreviation Harry with Henry (q.v.).

HARRIET *f.* (har′iet)

a feminine form of Henry (q.v.), from Harry, which was its usual form in the Middle Ages. It was also spelt Harriot. The name was at the height of its popularity between the 18th and 19th centuries. The usual pet form today is Hatty or Hattie.

HARRIOT *see* HARRIET

HARRY *see* HAROLD, HENRY

HARTLEY *m.* (hàt′li)

This surname was taken from a common place name derived from the Old English meaning 'deer pasture'. It is now quite often used as a Christian name.

HARUN, HAROUN, *see* AARON

HARVEY *m.* (hà′vi)

from the French meaning 'battle-worthy'. It may also have been used to transliterate the Saxon Harivig, after the

Norman Conquest. It remained common until the 14th century, and had a slight revival in the 19th. Its modern use as a Christian name may be due in part to its widespread use as a surname. It is more common as a Christian name in North America.

HATTIE, HATTY *see* HARRIET

HAZEL *f.* (hā′zel)

This is one of several plant names adopted as a girl's name in the 19th century. It is fairly common in Britain today.

HEATHER *f.* (heTH′e)

This is one of the plant names first used as a Christian name in the 19th century, and one of the more common ones today, especially in Scotland.

HEBE *f.* (hē′bi)

from the Greek meaning 'bloom of youth'. Hebe was the Greek goddess of youth and cupbearer to the gods, and appears in Homer's *Odyssey* as the

daughter of Zeus and Hera. The name
has been used occasionally in Britain,
but is rarely found today.

HECTOR m. (hek'tę)

from the Greek meaning 'hold fast'. It
was the name of the Trojan hero who
was killed by the Greek Achilles. 'Sir
Ector' became a hero of popular literature in the Middle Ages, and it was from
this that the general use of the name
arose. It took a strong hold in Scotland,
where it was used as an equivalent
for a quite unconnected Gaelic name
Eachan, meaning 'a horseman'.

HELEN f. (hel'ęn)

from Greek, meaning 'the bright one'.
The popularity of this name in Britain
was due originally to the 4th century
Saxon St. Helena. She was the mother
of Constantine the Great and was supposed to have been the daughter of the
Prince of Colchester, the Old King Cole
of nursery rhyme. When she was over
eighty she made a pilgrimage to the

Holy Land where she was believed to have found the true cross of Christ. The name is first found as Elena and then Elaine and Ellen. The 'h' was not used until the Renaissance, when the study of classical literature brought Homer's story of the Trojan war and the Greek queen Helen to public notice. Lena is a contraction of Helena. Helen is common in Scotland (*see* ELEANOR).

HELENA *see* HELEN

HELGA *f.* (hel'gĕ)

from the Norse meaning 'holy'. It has occasionally been used in Britain but is more common in North America, where it was introduced by Scandinavian immigrants (*see* OLGA).

HENRI, HENRICUS *see* HENRY

HENRIETTA *f.* (henriet'ĕ)

the feminine form of Henry (q.v.). It was introduced into this country in the 17th century by Henriette Marie, Charles I's French wife. The full form gave way to the abbreviated Harriet (q.v.), but was revived in the 19th century. Abbreviations are Etta and Hetty.

HENRIETTE *see* HENRIETTA

HENRY *m.* (*hen'ri*)

from the Old German meaning 'home ruler'. The Latin Henricus became Henri in France. It was very popular in the Middle Ages and has never entirely disappeared. Harry was, in fact, the original English form of Henri, used until the 17th century and often abbreviated to Hal. Today Harry is used as the pet form of Henry.

HERB *see* HERBERT

HERBERT *m.* (*her'bet*)

from the Old German meaning 'bright army'. It seldom appears before the Norman Conquest, after which it was reintroduced and became quite common. It was revived at the beginning of the 19th century, and became popular again towards the end of the century.

This latest revival was partly due to the fashion for adapting aristocratic surnames, but has also been attributed to the popularity of George Herbert's hymns. Herb and Bert or Bertie are short forms.

HERCULES m. (herk′ulēz)

This is the latinised form of the Greek Heracles, who was a famous hero in Greek mythology and is remembered for his twelve great feats of strength called labours. His name probably means 'glorious gift of Hera'; Hera was the queen of the Olympian gods. The name was used occasionally in Britain after the Renaissance and continued to be used in Cornwall and Shetland until the 19th century.

HEREWARD m. (her′ewed)

from the Old English meaning 'army protection'. A famous bearer of the name was the 11th century Saxon, Hereward the Wake, whose resistance to Norman rule was the basis of many tales of heroism, notably Charles Kingsley's novel *Hereward the Wake*. This 19th century work revived the name, but it is not common in the 20th century.

HERMIA *see* HERMIONE

HERMIONE *f.* (hẹrmi′oni)

from the Greek meaning 'daughter of Hermes' and in Greek mythology, the daughter of Menalaus and Helen. It was Shakespeare's use of the name in *A Winter's Tale* that gave rise to its use in modern times. He used another form, Hermia, in *A Midsummer Night's Dream*, and this also has been used from time to time.

HERNANDO *see* FERDINAND

HESTER *see* ESTHER

HETTY *see* HENRIETTA

HIERONYMOS *see* JEROME

HILARIUS *see* HILARY

HILARY, HILLARY *m. and f.* (hil'ẹri)

from the Latin meaning 'cheerful'. The name was popular in France due to the influence of St. Hilarius, a strong supporter of Christianity in the 4th century. It came to England in the Middle Ages and has been used occasionally ever since. It is becoming more common now as a girl's name.

HILDA *f.* (hil'dẹ)

from the Old English meaning 'battle'. There was an Anglo-Saxon St. Hilda who founded an abbey at Whitby in the 7th century. When the names of Anglo-Saxon saints were revived in the 19th century, Hilda became popular, and it is still in common use throughout Britain.

HIPPOLYTA *f.* (hipol'itẹ)

the feminine form of the Greek name Hippolytus (q.v.). In Greek legend, it was the name of the leader of the Amazons, a famous race of female warriors. It appears in Shakespeare's *A*

Midsummer Night's Dream, which is the most likely source of its modern use. It is not a common name.

HIPPOLYTUS *m.* (hipol'ites)

from the Greek meaning 'letting horses loose'. In Greek mythology, Hippolytus was the son of Hippolyta and Theseus, who was killed riding his chariot. There was a 3rd century saint and martyr of this name, and several churches have been dedicated to him. Hippolytus has never been commonly used in Britain but Hippolyte is quite common in France.

HIRAM *m.* (hī'rem)

from the Hebrew meaning 'brother' and 'high' or 'exalted', and the name of a king of Tyre in the Old Testament. It was a favourite name in the 17th century and was taken at that time to North America where the name still flourishes.

HODGE *see* ROGER

HONOR(I)(A) *f. (on'ẹ, onaw'rẹ, onaw'riẹ, honaw'riẹ)*

from the Latin meaning 'reputation' or 'honour'. The Latin forms Honora, Honoria and Annora were predominant till the Reformation, when the Puritans adopted abstract virtue names and used Honour and Honor. They were then used both as masculine and feminine names. In the 19th century the Latin forms came back briefly. At the moment Honor is most popular, and it is an exclusively feminine name.

HONORIUS *see* **ANEURIN**

HONOUR *see* **HONOR**

HOPE *m. and f. (hōp)*

This Christian quality was adopted as a Christian name in the 17th century, like Honour, Faith, Charity, etc. It was especially popular among Puritans at this time. It is still used fairly widely for either sex.

HORACE, HORATIO *m.* (*hor'ęs, horă'shio*)

from the Latin clan named Horatius, of which the famous Roman soldier, Horatius Cocles, was a member. The fame of the name is also due to the Latin poet Horace who adopted it. Horatio seems to have come from Italy to England in the 16th century. Horace is the form which is most often used today, though the 1st Viscount Nelson made the Horatio form well-known. Horatia is a rare feminine form.

HORATIA, HORATIUS *see* HORACE

HORTENSIA *f.* (*hawtens'ię*)

from a Roman clan name. Ortensia, the Italian form, was adopted in France as Hortense in the 17th century and, like many other French names, has fluctuated in popularity throughout Britain, never becoming very common.

HOWARD *m.* (*how'ęd*)

Like other aristocratic family names this

was adopted as a Christian name by the general public in the 19th century. The origin of the surname is disputed. It may be from Old German meaning 'heart-protection' or the French for 'worker with a hoe', or even from the medieval official the 'Hogwarden' who superintended the pigs of a district. It is a common Christian name in Britain today.

HRODLAND see **ROLAND**

HRODULF see **RUDOLF**

HROTHGAR see **ROGER**

HUBERT m. (hū′bẹt)

from the Old German meaning 'heart bright'. This name was very popular in the Middle Ages, probably as a result of the fame of St. Hubert of Liège, the patron saint of huntsmen. It was not used from the 15th-19th centuries, after which it was revived to some extent.

HUGH, HUGO *m.* (hū', hū'gō)

from the Old German meaning 'heart' or 'soul'. It was brought to Britain by the Normans and appears frequently in Domesday Book. It was further strengthened by the popularity of St. Hugh, Bishop of Lincoln in the 14th century. Hugo is the Latin form, and both are still quite common, Hugh being used as a transliteration of certain Gaelic names in Scotland and Ireland.

HUMBERT *m.* (hum'bẹt)

from the Old German meaning 'giant bright'. The name is very common in Italy in the form Umberto, but is rather rare in Britain.

HUMPHREY *m.* (hum'fri)

from the Old English meaning 'giant peace'. This name was originally spelt with an 'f', the 'ph' coming in when it was equated with the name of the Egyptian St. Onuphrios in order to Christianise it. The name appears in the Old English period, and its popularity was reinforced by the Norman Conquest. At first it was confined to the nobility but later its use became general. As a result of becoming too common, it fell out of favour, but was revived in the 19th century and is still often found.

HUNTER *m.* (*hun'tę*)

from Old English for 'a hunter'. This is sometimes used as a Christian name, possibly in connection with the surname, which is far more common.

I

IAN, IAIN *see* JOHN

IDA *f.* (*ī'dę*)

from the Old German meaning 'hard work'. The name was introduced by the Normans, and lasted until about the middle of the 14th century. Tennyson's poem *The Princess* and Gilbert and Sullivan's opera *Princess Ida*, were based on it, and led to a revival of the name at the end of the 19th century.

IDRIS *m.* (*id'ris*)

This is a popular Welsh name meaning 'fiery lord'. In Welsh legend Idris the Giant was an astronomer and magician, who had his observatory on Cader Idris.

IGNATIUS *m.* (*ignā'shĕs*)

This is a Latin name, derived originally from a Greek name of obscure origin. It is used mainly by Catholics in this country, but most often takes the form Inigo (q.v.).

ILONA *f.* (*ilō'nĕ*)

This is a rare name derived from the Hungarian meaning 'beautiful one'. It has been suggested that it is a variant form of Helen (q.v.).

ILSABETH *see* ISABEL

IMOGEN *f.* (*im'ŏjĕn*)

First appearing in Shakespeare's *Cymbeline*, this name is thought to be a misprint of the Innogen which appears in Holinshed, Shakespeare's source for the story.

The medieval historian, Geoffrey of Monmouth also uses the name, but its etymology is uncertain. It may be derived from the Greek meaning 'beloved child'.

INES, INEZ *see* **AGNES**

ING *see* **INGRAM, INGRID**

INGELRAM, INGERAM *see* **INGRAM**

INGRAM m. (*in'grem*)

from the Old German meaning 'Ing's raven'. The name developed from the Old English Ingelram, which later became Ingeram. Ing was an ancient Norse deity who was regarded by the Angles as their ancestor. It is regarded as significant by some scholars that England is pronounced *ing'land* and not *eng'land*. The name was used up to the end of the 19th century. Its use in the 19th and 20th centuries is usually in connection with the common surname.

INGRID *m.* (*ing'rid*)

from the Old Norse meaning 'Ing's ride'. Ing in Norse mythology was the god of fertility and crops and his steed was a golden bristled boar. The name is common in Scandinavia but, apart from isolated examples in the Middle Ages, it has only recently been used in Britain. This may be partly due to the popularity of the Swedish film star Ingrid Bergman in this country.

INIGO *m.* (*in'igō*)

from Greek but of obscure meaning, possible meaning 'fiery'. The 1st century Bishop of Antioch of this name was by tradition the author of the Epistles to the Romans and Ephesians. The name took root mainly in Russia and Spain. It was carried further afield by the Jesuits whose founder was Inigo Lopez de Recalde or St. Ignatius de Loyola, as he was popularly known. The name has been used mainly by Roman Catholics in this country. The best known holder of the name in Britain was Inigo Jones, the 17th century architect.

INNOGEN *see* IMOGEN

IOLA *f.* (ī′ōlẹ)

from the Greek meaning 'dawn cloud'. In Greek mythology Hercules fell in love a princess Iole and captured her. The name is rare in Britain.

IONA *f.* (īō′nẹ)

from the Greek meaning 'violet coloured stone'. In Scotland the Christian name is usually taken from the name of the Hebridean island. Ione is also used.

IOR *see* IVOR

IRENE *f.* (īrēn′, īrē′ni)

from the Greek meaning 'peace', and the name of the goddess of peace in ancient Greece. Although the name was used earlier in other parts of Europe, it was not used in England until the late 19th century. It is now very common. The original pronunciation was īrē′ni, but the American $īrēn'$ is now more popular in Britain also. The abbreviation Renie is sometimes used.

IRIS f. ($ī'ris$)

Although this name is usually associated with the flower, it comes from the Greek word for 'rainbow', after which the flower was named, because of its bright colours. In Greek mythology Iris carried messages from the gods to men, across the rainbow which was her bridge. It was not used in England before the 19th century, but is now fairly popular.

IRVING m. ($er'ving$)

The origin of this name is disputed. It is either from Old English Earwine, meaning 'sea friend' or Old Welsh Erwyn, meaning 'white river'. The modern use of the name may have been influenced by its use as a surname. Modern examples are Irving Berlin, the composer, and Irving Stone, the author.

ISA see ISABEL

ISAAC, IZAAK m. (ī′zek)

from the Hebrew meaning 'laughter'.
It was the name given by Sarah, wife
of Abraham, to the son born in her old
age. The name is popularly believed
to have been chosen by Sarah because
she laughed when she was told that
she would conceive. The name appears
in Britain in the Middle Ages, but it
came to be regarded as a specifically
Jewish name. The name came into
general use in the 16th and 17th centuries, when it was spelt with a 'z'
as in Izaak Walton, the author of *The
Compleat Angler*. In the mid 17th century the 's' spelling came into vogue,
as in Sir Isaac Newton, the great
scientist. The name is uncommon today,
except among Jews.

ISABEL(LA), ISOBEL f. (izɐbel′(ɐ), iz′obel)

These variants of Elizabeth (q.v.) seem
to have originated in medieval France.
Elizabeth became Ilsabeth and then
Isabeau, and finally Isabelle. Up to the

end of the 17th century at least, the derivatives Isabel(le) in England, Isobel in Scotland and the Gaelic Iseabail, sometimes transliterated as Ishbel, were interchangeable with Elizabeth. Isa and Bel(le) were the common short forms, and the latinised Isabella and Bella were used in the 18th and 19th centuries.

ISAIAH *m. (īzi'ę)*

from the Hebrew meaning 'Jehovah is generous', and the name of the great Old Testament prophet. It was first used by the 17th century Puritans, and is rather rare today in Britain, although slightly more common in North America.

ISEABAIL *see* **ISABEL**

ISHBEL *see* **ISABEL**

ISIDORE, ISIDORA *f. (iz'idaw, izidaw'rę)*

from Greek, possibly meaning 'gift of Isis'. The name was not uncommon in ancient Greece. There were two Spanish saints of this name and it was taken up by the Spanish Jews. The name spread to Jews in this country, and has been used, rarely from the mid 17th century.

ISOLDA *f.* (*izōl'dẹ*)

possibly from Old Welsh Essylt, meaning 'fair one' or Old German Isvald, meaning 'ice rule'. It was a common name in medieval times because of its place in Arthurian legend. Iseult was the Norman form which became Isolda in Latin, Isot(t) in Middle English. Isolda had a brief revival in the 19th century owing to the popularity of Wagner's opera *Tristan and Isolde*.

ISRAEL *m.* (*iz'rāl*)

from Hebrew. The meaning is disputed but the most likely translation is 'may God prevail'. In the Old Testament Jacob was named Israel because of his struggle with the angel of God. The name was first adopted by Christians after the Reformation. It continued in use, mostly among the poorer classes, until the late 19th century. It has always been used as a given name among Jews.

IVAN *m.* (ĭv′ẹn, ĕván′)

the Russian form of John (q.v.) which is occasionally found in Britain.

IVO *m.* (ĭ′vō)

from the Old German meaning 'yew'. It was common in Brittany in the form Yves, and was brought to Britain at the time of the Norman Conquest. It has been used very occasionally since.

IVOR, IFOR *m.* (ĭ′vẹ, ĕ′faw)

Ifor is a Welsh name which means 'lord', and Ivor is the anglicised spelling. It was originally Ior, but was probably influenced by the similar Breton Yves, which became Ivo (q.v.) and was brought over by the Normans in this form. Today Ivor is the common form, but Ifor is still used in Wales, and Ivo has enjoyed a small revival in the 20th century.

IVY *f.* (*ī′vi*)

This is a plant name coined in the 19th century, which, perhaps because of its capacity for clinging, may signify faithfulness.

J

JACK *m.* (*jak*)

Originally the pet form of John (q.v.), this is now a well-known independent name. It was formed from the Flemish diminutive Jankins, from which the 'n' was omitted in Britain. It was so common in the Middle Ages that it became a synonym for a man, and most of the popular uses of the word are derived from this. Jock is a particularly Scottish variant.

JACKY *see* **JACQUELINE**

JACOB *m.* (*jā′kẹb*)

Originally Hebrew, the meaning of this name is uncertain. In the Old Testament it was the name of Isaac's younger son, who tricked his brother, Esau, out of his inheritance. This explains the popular interpretation of the name as 'he supplanted'. There were two Latin forms, Jacobus and Jacomus. Jacob came from the former and James from the latter. Jacob has survived as a Christian name because the translators of the Bible kept this form for the Old Testament Patriarch, although they called the two New Testament apostles James. Jacob was common after the Reformation, but in modern times has not enjoyed anything like the popularity of James. Jacoba and Jacobina are rare feminine forms. Jake is an abbreviation.

JACOBA, JACOBINA see **JACOB**

JACOBUS, JACOMUS see **JACOB**

JACQUELINE, JACQUETTA f.
(*jak'elin, jaket'e*)

These are French diminutives of Jacques, the French equivalent of James and Jacob (q.v.). Both were introduced into this country from Belgium in the 13th century, and have been in use ever since. Jacqueline, with the pet form Jacky, is the more popular of the two today.

JACQUES *see* JACQUELINE

JAKE *see* JACOB

JAMES m. (*jāmz*)

This name has the same root as Jacob (q.v.). It became established in Britain in the 12th century, when pilgrims started to visit the shrine of St. James, the son of Zebedee, at Compostella in Spain. At that time the name was more common in Scotland. With the accession of James Stuart as first king of both England and Scotland, the name began to increase in popularity in England, in the 17th century. It was unfashionable in the 19th century, when it was used as a general term for a man servant, but is now more popular than ever. The pet forms are Jim and Jimmy, and in Scotland Jamie is also used. The Irish form is Seumus (*shā'męs*). Jamesina is a rare Scottish feminine form.

JAMIE *see* JAMES

JAN *see* JANET

JAN *m.* (*jan*)

This is a variant form of (*q.v.*) John, originating in the West Country. Its use has now spread into other parts of Britain.

JANE *f.* (*jān*)

This is now the commonest feminine form of John (q.v.). It is derived from the Old French form Jehane. It was very rare before the 16th century, the medieval feminine forms of John being Joan and Joanna (qq.v.). An early example was Jane Seymour, Henry VIII's third wife, and mother of Edward VI. Since Tudor times the name has been in and out of fashion, until, in the 20th century, it has become one of the commonest of all girls' names.

In the 18th and early 19th centuries it was often combined with another name, e.g. Sarah Jane (which was sometimes pronounced *sejān*). Sine, sometimes with the English spelling Sheena, is the Gaelic version. Janice is a variant which is popular today. The commonest pet forms are Jenny and Janey (*see* JANET).

JANET *f.* (*jan'et*)

This was originally derived from Jeanette the French diminutive of Jean (q.v.). It is a particularly Scottish variant which is now given as a separate name. Janette and Janetta are also found, and Nettie, Netta and Jan are pet names. A Scottish diminutive is Jessie (q.v.).

JANETTA, JANETTE *see* JANET

JANEY, JANICE *see* JANE

JANKIN(S) *see* JACK

JASMINE *f.* (*jas'min*)

from Persian *yasaman*, meaning 'the

jasmine flower'. Jessamine and Jessamyn are further anglicised forms, and Jasmina has the Latin ending. All of these have been used from time to time in different parts of Britain.

JASON *m.* (*jā'sęn*)

This name was adopted in the 17th century when Biblical names became popular. It is the name given for the author of *Ecclesiasticus*. Jason was a translation of the Greek which in turn represented some Hebrew name, probably Joshua (q.v.).

JASPAR, CASPAR *m.* (*jas'pę, kas'pę*)

Gaspar or Caspar was believed to have been the name of one of the three kings or 'wise men' of the Christmas story. His name may mean 'keeper' or 'bringer of treasure'. Gaspard is the French form and Jasper the English. Both names are still used from time to time.

JEAN *f.* (*jēn*)

a Scottish form of Jane or Joan (qq.v.)

derived from the Old French Jehane. It is a very popular name throughout Britain. The diminutive Jeanette is also found (see JANET). The commonest pet forms are Jeanie and Jenny.

JEANETTE *see* JANET, JEAN

JEFF *see* GEOFFREY

JEFFREY *see* GEOFFREY

JEHANE *see* JANE

JEMIMA *f.* (*jemī'mę*)

from the Hebrew meaning 'dove', and the name of one of Job's daughters in the Old Testament. It was first used in the 17th century by Puritans, and was very popular in the 19th century. It may have been used as a feminine form of James.

JEN(N)IFER *f.* (*jen'ifę*)

Jennifer was an old Cornish form of Guenevere, from the Welsh meaning 'fair and yielding', which was the name of King Arthur's wife. It was practically obsolete when it was revived in the 20th century. It spread rapidly, and is now very popular throughout Britain. Jenny is the pet form.

JENNY *see* JANE, JEAN, JENNIFER

JEREMIAS *see* JEREMY

JEREMY, JEREMIAH *m.* (*jer'emi, jeremī'e*)

from the Hebrew meaning 'may Jehovah exalt'. Jeremiah was the Old Testament prophet who wrote the *Book of Lamentations*. The traditional English form is Jeremy, which appears from the 13th century onwards, and is very popular at present. In the 17th century the two forms Jeremias and Jeremiah were common. Jerry is the short form, which is shared with Gerald (q.v.).

JEROME *m.* (*jerōm'*)

from the Greek Hieronymos, meaning 'holy name'. This name is pre-Christian in origin, but soon became popular with the early Church because of its association with the Lord's Prayer. St. Jerome, who bore the Latin form Hieronymus, translated the Bible into Latin in the 4th century, and was an important religious influence in the Middle Ages. The name appears in England in the 12th century as Geronimus, which gradually gave way to the French form Jérôme. A famous modern holder of the name is Jerome K. Jerome who wrote *Three Men in a Boat*.

JERRY, GERRY *see* JEREMY, GERALD

JESS, JESSIE *see* JESSICA

JESSE *m. (jes'i)*

from the Hebrew meaning 'God exists', and, in the Old Testament, the name of King David's father. It was adopted in the 17th century by the Puritans, who took it to America, where it has been commoner than in this country. Jesse James, the mid-19th century American outlaw, is probably the best known example.

JESSICA f. (jes'ikə)

from the Hebrew meaning 'God beholds'. Its use in Britain is probably due to the influence of Shakespeare's play, *The Merchant of Venice*, in which Shylock's daughter is called Jessica. It is still a fairly popular name, often shortened to Jesse or Jessie.

JESSIE f. (jes'i)

This is a Scottish diminutive of Janet (q.v.), but it is often used as a separate name. It is fairly common in the literature of the 18th and 19th centuries, and is also a pet form of Jessica (q.v.).

JETHRO m. (jeth'rō)

from the Hebrew meaning 'abundance' or 'excellence'. It has occasionally been used as a Christian name since the Reformation. A well-known example is Jethro Tull, the 18th century agricultural reformer.

JHONE *see* **JOAN**

JILL f. (jil)

a pet form of Gillian or Jillian (q.v.), often given as a separate name.

JILLIAN see GILLIAN

JIM, JIMMY see JAMES

JO, JOE see JOSEPH, JOSEPHINE

JOAN f. (jōn)

This is the oldest English feminine form of John (q.v.), and is a contraction of Johanna, the Latin feminine form of Johannes. The name came over from France as Jhone and Johan in the second half of the 12th century, but by the 14th century Joan was the established form. By the mid-16th century it was so common that it became unfashionable, and Jane (q.v.) superseded it. It was revived at the beginning of the 20th century, and is again very popular (see JOANNA).

JOANNA f. (jōan'ę)

Johanna was the medieval Latin feminine form of Johannes (*see* JOHN). Both it and Johanna, which is how it is rendered in the Authorised Version of the New Testament, (Luke XXIV, 20) were adopted in the 18th century. Joanna has been revived in the 20th century, and is once again a popular name. Juanita is the Spanish diminutive, which, with its short form Nita is also found in Britain.

JOB *m.* (*jŏb*)

from the Hebrew meaning 'hated' or 'persecuted'. The medieval use of the name may have had an Old German origin, but it was certainly used in its Biblical context after the Reformation. It has never been common.

JOCELYN, JOCELIN *m. and f.* (*jos'(e-)lin*)

probably from the Latin meaning 'gay', 'sportive'. There is also a possibility that it is derived from an old German name. A further derivation has been traced from the name Josse, a form of Jodoc, the name of an early Breton saint. It is an uncommon name today.

JOCK *see* **JACK, JOHN**

JODOC *see* **JOCELYN**

JODOCUS *see* **JOYCE**

JOEL *m.* (jō′ẹl)

from the Hebrew meaning 'Jehovah is God', and the name of one of the minor Old Testament prophets. It was adopted by Puritans, like many other Biblical names, after the Reformation. Its earlier use in the Middle Ages was derived from the name of a Breton saint, Juhel.

JOHAN *see* **JOAN, JOHN**

JOHANE *see* **JEAN**

JOHANNES *see* **JOHN**

JOHN *m.* (jon)

from the Hebrew meaning 'the Lord is gracious' or 'Grace of the Lord'. This name was a favourite in the Eastern Church. The Crusaders brought it back to England, where it began to spread in the 12th century. Its earliest form in Europe was the Latin Johannes, which was shortened to Johan and Jon, and hence John. A particularly Scottish variant form is Jock (*see* JACK). Ian and Iain are the Gaelic forms, Evan the Welsh, and Sean the Irish. From the 16th century onwards, John became predominant as a boy's name, and it is still one of the commonest boys' names in Britain.

JOISSE *see* **JOYCE**

JOLYON *see* **JULIAN**

JON *see* **JOHN**

JONAH, JONAS *m.* (*jō′nẹ, jō′nẹs*)

from the Hebrew meaning 'dove'. The story of Jonah and the whale in the Old Testament was very popular in the Middle Ages and, because of this, the name was common. It was revived after the Reformation, and was used occasionally until the 19th century, when it died out. Jonas (q.v.) was the Greek form, which was used in the 12th and 13th centuries.

JONATHAN m. (*jon'ethen*)

from the Hebrew meaning 'the Lord has given'. In the Old Testament, Jonathan was the son of King Saul and it was his great friendship with David that gave rise to the expression 'David and Jonathan' to describe two close friends. The name was taken into use at the time of the Reformation, and it is quite common today.

JOSCELIN f. (*jos'elin*)

This name came to be given to girls only recently, after centuries of use as a boy's name in the form Jocelyn (q.v.). It has been suggested, however, that Joscelin has a different origin, being derived from a Latin word meaning 'just'. It is not a common name in Britain today.

JOSEPH m. (*jō'zef, jō'sef*)

from the Hebrew meaning 'the Lord added' (i.e. to the family). In the Old

Testament it was the name of Jacob and Rachel's elder son who was sold into slavery in Egypt. In the New Testament, there were Joseph, the husband of Mary, and Joseph of Arimathea, who is believed to have buried Jesus, and whom legend connects with Glastonbury and the Holy Grail. The name was not frequently used until the 17th century, when Old Testament names were adopted by the Puritans, and Joseph became a favourite. Joe and Jo are common abbreviations.

JOSEPHINE f. (jō'zefēn, jō'sefēn)

This was originally a pet form of Josephe, the French form of Josepha, which is the feminine of the Latin Josephus (*see* JOSEPH). It was Napoleon's first wife, the Empress Josephine, who started the fashion for the name in Britain and France. Josepha was also used in the 19th century. Pet forms are Jo(e) and Josie.

JOSH *see* JOSHUA

JOSHUA *m.* (*josh'ūę*)

from the Hebrew meaning 'the Lord is generous'. In the Old Testament Joshua succeeded Moses and finally led the Israelites to the Promised Land. The name was not used in England before the Reformation. Its most famous British bearer was Sir Joshua Reynolds, the painter, who was appointed the first President of the Royal Academy by George III. Josh is a popular short form, especially in North America, where the name is commoner than in Britain.

JOSIAH *m.* (*jōzī'ę*)

from the Hebrew meaning 'may the Lord heal'. It was most common in the 17th century. The famous 18th century potter, Josiah Wedgwood, in whose family the name is still used, is possibly the best known British bearer of the name.

JOSIE *see* **JOSEPHINE**

JOSSE *see* **JOCELYN, JOYCE**

JOY *f.* (*joi*)

This is just the word 'joy', taken from Latin, used as a Christian name. It occurs as early as the 12th century, and was revived in the 19th century. It is now quite common.

JOYCE *m. and f.* (*jois*)

In the Middle Ages, when this name was most common, it usually had the form Josse. A 7th century saint from Brittany, whose name was latinised to Jodocus, was the cause of the name's popularity. One of the French variants of the name was Joisse, and it was from this that the final form of the name was derived. It was dropped as a man's name in the 14th century, but as a girl's name it survived, and has had something of a revival in the 20th century.

JUANITA *see* JOANNA

JUDAS *see* JUDE

JUDE *m.* (*jōōd*)

The Hebrew form of this name is

Yehudi, which was rendered as Judah in the Authorised Version of the Old Testament. Judas Iscariot bore the Greek form, and because of him the name was never used by Christians until the Reformation. Jude was used in the Authorised Version to distinguish the author of *The Epistle of Jude*. The name has been used occasionally, and is best known through Thomas Hardy's novel *Jude the Obscure*.

JUDITH f. (*jōō'dith*)

from the Hebrew meaning 'a Jewess', and, in the Old Testament, the name of Esau's wife. The name appears both before and after the Norman Conquest, but did not become common until the 17th century. The short-form Judy is often given independently.

JUDY see JUDITH

JUHEL see JOEL

JULIA f. (*jōō'liə*)

This is the feminine form of Julius (q.v.),

which came to England from Italy as Giulia in the 16th century, and was used by Shakespeare in *Two Gentlemen of Verona*. It did not become common in Britain until the 18th and 19th centuries (*see* JULIANA, JULIET).

JULIAN m. (*jōō'liən*)

Latin Julianus, derived from Julius (q.v.) The most famous of numerous saints of this name was St. Julian the Hospitaller, who devoted himself to helping poor travellers. The name came to Britain in the 13th century in the Latin form, which was anglicised as Julyan, and in the North of England as Jolyon. Julian became popular in the 19th century, and today is quite a common name.

JULIAN, JULIANA f. (*jōō'liən, jōōliān'ę*)

These are both feminine forms of Julian (q.v.). St. Juliana was an early Christian martyr, whose relics are said to have been taken to Brussels, and it has been suggested that the name first came to

Britain in the 12th century from the Low Countries. A prioress in St. Albans, whose name was Julian or Juliana wrote a treatise on field sports in the 15th century, and in the same century Julyan of Norwich wrote *Revelations of Divine Love*. The variant forms Gillian (q.v.) and Jill were among the commonest girl's names from the 12th to the 15th centuries. The name subsequently dropped out of popular use, but was revived in the 18th century. Gillian is probably the most popular form today. It shares the short form Julie with Juliet (q.v.) (*see* JULIA).

JULIANUS *see* JULIAN

JULIE *see* JULIANA, JULIET

JULIET *f.* (*jōō′liet*)

This is a short form of the Italian Giulietta, a diminutive of Julia (q.v.). Its use nowadays is probably the result of the influence of Shakespeare's *Romeo and Juliet*. Juliette is a French form sometimes used in Britain, as is Julie, an abbreviation of either form, which is also a name in its own right today.

JULIETTE *see* JULIET

JULIUS *m.* (*jōō'liŭs*)

the name of the Roman clan to which Caius Julius Caesar belonged. The meaning of the name is not certain, since, although it can be translated as 'hairy', this might be in the Greek sense of 'downy bearded', and hence 'clean-shaven'. The name has never been used much in Britain, but there was a judge named Julius Caesar who was knighted in 1603, and his family continued the tradition of combining the two names. Today Julian (q.v.), a derivative, is far more common.

JULYAN *see* JULIAN, JULIANA

JUNE *f.* (*jōōn*)

This is simply the name of the month which, like April, has been used as a girl's name in the 20th century.

JUNO *see* UNA

JUSTIN *m.* (*jus'tin*)

from the Latin meaning 'just'. It was the name of two Byzantine emperors, and has been used occasionally in modern times.

JUSTINA *see* **JUSTINE**

JUSTINE *f.* (*justēn'*)

the feminine form of Justin (q.v.). Another feminine form which is occasionally found is Justina.

K

KAREL *see* **CAROL**

KAREN *see* **KATHERINE**

KATE, KATIE *see* **KATHERINE**

KATHARINE, KATHERINE, CATHARINE, CATHERINE *f.* (*kath'rin*)

from Greek *katharos*, meaning 'pure'. The name came to England in the early 12th century when crusaders brought back the legend of St. Katharine of Alexandria. She was an Egyptian princess who was tortured and put to death in the early 4th century, for her learned defence of Christianity. The legend and the name became very popular in Britain, and today it is one of the commonest of all girl's names. The most common short forms have been Kate, Kitty, Katie and recently Cathy and Kay (*see* KAY *m.*). The Irish form Kathleen or Cathleen is now used throughout Britain. Catriona (*katre'one̜*) is the Gaelic diminutive, and the Danish Karen has also been borrowed recently.

KATHLEEN *see* **KATHARINE**

KAY *see* **KATHARINE**

KAY *m. and f.* (*kā*)

The origin of this name is disputed. It may be a variant of the Latin name Caius, or it may come from Welsh or Irish words, meaning respectively 're-joicer' and 'fiery'. Sir Kay is one of the more famous knights of the round table, of Arthurian Legend. The name is now more common as the shortened form of the girl's name, Katherine (q.v.).

KEITH *m.* (*kēth*)

This is a popular Christian name from Scotland which has spread throughout Britain. It is taken from the Scottish place name, which is probably derived from the Gaelic for 'wood' or 'windy place'.

KEN, KENNY *see* KENNETH

KENELM *m.* (*ken'elm*)

from Old English, meaning 'brave helmet'. The 9th century martyr, St. Kenelm, King of Mercia, was venerated in the Midlands, where the Christian name flourished and is still in use.

KENNETH *m.* (*ken'eth*)

an anglicised derivative of the Gaelic Coinneach, meaning 'handsome', and equivalent to modern Welsh Cenydd. This is basically a Scottish name which became popular when Kenneth Mac-

Alpine became 1st King of Scotland in the 9th century, uniting the Picts and the Scots. From Scotland it gradually spread over Britain. It is often shortened to Ken or Kenny.

KESTER see CHRISTOPHER

KEVIN m. (ke'vin)

from the Irish meaning 'handsome birth'. This name is very popular in Ireland on account of St. Kevin, a 6th century hermit, who later became abbot of Glendalough. It is in fairly common use throughout Britain.

KIM m. and f. (kim)

probably from Old English *cynebeald*. meaning 'royally bold', through the surname Kimball. Rudyard Kipling's hero in the novel *Kim* (1901) used a shortened form of his true name, Kimball O'Hara, showing the use of the surname as a Christian name. More recently the name has been almost exclusively used for girls.

KIRSTY *see* **CHRISTIANA**

KIT *see* **CHRISTOPHER**

KITTY *see* **KATHARINE**

KLAUS *see* **NICHOLAS**

KORDEL, KORDULA *see* **CORDELIA**

L

LACHLAN *m.* (*laH'len*)

from Gaelic meaning 'warlike'. Lochlann is Gaelic for Norway. This is primarily a Highland name.

LAETITIA *see* **LETTICE**

LAMBERT *m.* (*lam'bet*)

from the Old German meaning 'land famous'. The name was common in England from the 12th to the 15th centuries. It was brought over by Flemish weavers from the Low Countries, where the name was popular because of the 7th century St. Lambert, Bishop of Maastricht. In Britain, it is best known for Lambert Simnel, who tried to oust Henry VII from the throne. Due to this famous pretender, the name went out of favour. It has been used occasionally since the 19th century.

LANCE, LANCELIN see LANCELOT

LANCELOT m. (làn'sęlot)

possibly a variant of the French Lance, from the Old German for 'land'. Both forms, and also Lancelin, were used in Britain from the 13th century, but only Lancelot survived. This was due to the popularity of Sir Lancelot in the stories of King Arthur. The name is more often found in its short form, Lance, today.

LARRIE, LAURIE see LAURENCE

LAURA, LAURETTA f. (law'rę, lawret'ę)

Laura is derived, like Lawrence (q.v.), from the Latin for 'laurel', a symbol, in the classical world, of victory and poetic genius. Lauretta is the diminutive form. Together with Laurencia and Lora these names were common from the 12th century. Today Laura is the most popular, and Lora, with its diminutive Loretta, is less frequently used. Other diminutives which are sometimes used are Laureen, Laurene, and Laurissa.

LAURENCE, LAWRENCE *m.* *(lor'ens)*

from the Latin meaning 'of Laurentium', a town which took its name from the laurel plant, symbol of victory. It became common in the 12th century. St. Laurence, the 3rd century Archdeacon of Rome, was a favourite medieval saint. It was popular in Ireland because of St. Laurence O'Toole, a 12th century Archbishop of Dublin, whose real name was Lorcan. Larrie is the usual abbreviation in England, while Laurie is used in Scotland. Such surnames as Laurie, Lowrie, Lawson and Larkin are derivatives. Additional fame was given to the name in the 20th century by the exploits and writings of Lawrence of Arabia.

LAURENCIA, LAUREEN, LAURENE, LAURISSA *see* LAURA

LAVINIA *f.* (lẹvin'iẹ)

The meaning of this name is unknown, but in classical legend it was the name of Aeneas' wife, for whose hand he fought and defeated a rival suitor. The town Lavinium, originally called Latium, was renamed after her. The name was very popular for a while during the Renaissance, but then faded out, only returning to fashion in the 18th century. It is still used occasionally.

LEILA *f.* (lē'lẹ)

a Persian name meaning 'dark-haired'. Byron started the fashion for it in the 19th century by using it in a poem with an oriental setting called *The Giaour*. The name appeared in the Persian romantic legend of Leilah and Mejnoun, equivalent to the story of Cupid and Psyche of the Greeks. It is now fairly popular.

LEILAH *see* LEILA

LEN, LENNIE, LENNY
see **LEONARD**

LENA *see* **HELEN**

LEO m. (*lē'ō*)

from the Latin meaning 'lion'. It was the name of six Emperors of Constantinople and of thirteen Popes, and is popular among Roman Catholics. Léon and Lyon were fairly common medieval forms. The French Léon is today a common Jewish name. Leo is occasionally used in this country and Rider Haggard gave the name to the hero of *She*, Leo Vincey. Leonie (*leōn'i*) is the feminine form of Léon, which is gaining popularity.

LEOLIN, LEOLINE *see* **LLEWELYN**

LÉON *see* **LEO, LIONEL**

LEONARD m. (*len'ĕd*)

from the Old German meaning 'lion brave'. The 6th century St. Leonhard was a Frankish nobleman who was converted to Christianity. He became a hermit, and devoted his life to helping prisoners, of whom he is the patron saint. His popularity made the name common in medieval England and France. The name was revived in the 19th century and is now fairly common. The usual shortened forms are Len, Lennie and Lenny.

LEONHARD see LEONARD

LEONIE see LEO

LEONORA, LENORE, LEONORE *f.*
(*lēonaw'rę, lenaw', lęo'naw*)

These names are European derivatives of Eleanor (q.v.), all of which have been used from time to time in this country. None of them appeared in Britain before the 19th century and their introduction was probably due to literary and musical influences. None of them have survived to any great extent. A short form which is fairly common is Nora (q.v.).

LEOPOLD m. (lĕ'epōld)

from the Óld German meaning 'people bold'. This name came to Britain through Queen Victoria's uncle, King Leopold of Belgium, after whom she named her fourth son, the Duke of Albany. It has not been used much in the 20th century.

LESLIE, LESLEY m. and f. (lez'li)

These are respectively the usual masculine and feminine spellings of the name. It is a Scottish surname used originally by the Lords of Leslie in Aberdeenshire. It was taken into general use as a Christian name in the late 19th century.

LESTER m. (les'tẹ)

This is a surname of uncertain etymology, which is sometimes used as a Christian name. Famous modern examples are Lester Pearson, the Canadian statesman, and Lester Piggott the English jockey.

LETTICE, L(A)ETITIA *f.* (*let'is,* *letish'ę*)

from the Latin meaning 'gladness'. Lettice was the usual form of this name from the 12th to the 17th centuries, during which time it was very popular. In the 18th century the Latin Laetitia superseded it, sometimes reduced to Letitia. None of these names are particularly common at present, though Lettice did return briefly in the late 19th and early 20th century.

LEWIS, LOUIS *m.* (*lŏŏ'is, lŏŏ'i*)

from Old German Chlodowig, meaning 'famous warrior', which was latinised into Ludovicus, and, in the French form, Clovis, was the name of the founder of the French monarchy. Clovis became Louis, and this was the name of eighteen French Kings. The Normans brought the name to England where it became Lewis and sometimes Lowis. The use of the French Louis is comparatively recent; Robert Louis Stevenson is an early example, and this form is quite common in the lowlands of Scotland. In Wales, Lewis has been used to anglicise Llewelyn (q.v.).

LIBBY *see* ELIZABETH

LIESEL *see* ELIZABETH

LILIAN, LILY *f.* (*lil'iən, lil'i*)

Originally these names may have been pet forms of Elizabeth (q.v.). Lillian is found in Shakespeare's time but the name was probably associated with the Lily flower even then. In the 19th century Lily was definitely given as the name of the flower, which is a Christian symbol of purity. Lil is the usual abbreviation. In Scotland the form Lillias is also found.

LILITH *f.* (*lil'ith*)

from the Hebrew meaning either 'serpent' or 'belonging to night'. In semitic mythology Lilith was an evil spirit who haunted the night and who had been Adam's rejected wife before Eve. The name has been used very rarely.

LINDA, LINDY *see* BELINDA

LINDA *f.* (*lin'de*)

This was a common ending for girls' names in Old German, and comes from the word for a snake, an animal which was held in great reverence by primitive Germanic tribes. Its attributed qualities were wisdom and suppleness, and the names derived from it were therefore complimentary. In Spanish *linda* means pretty, and this may also have had some effect on the use of Linda as an English Christian name, which only dates from the 19th century. It is also used as a contraction of Belinda (q.v.).

LINDSEY *m. and f.* (*lin'zi*)

from the Old English meaning 'pool island'. Together with its other forms Lindsay, Linsey, and Linsay, this name is used for both boys and girls. It is also common as a surname.

LINETTE *f.* (*linet'*)

from the Latin for 'flax'. This name for
the small flax-eating bird, is the Old
French form, rendered in English as
Linnet. The name is well known in
Britain through the story of the lovers
Gareth and Lynette, in Arthurian legend,
and in Tennyson's *Idylls of the King*.
It is often found in the short form Lynn
(q.v.) which is also a name in its own
right.

LIONEL *m.* (*lī'oneI*)

a French diminutive of Léon, meaning
'young lion'. It was the name of one of
King Arthur's knights and was given
by Edward III to his third son, later
Duke of Clarence. The name was
popular in the Middle Ages and survived in the North of England, whence
it has come back into general, though
infrequent use (*see* LEO).

LISA *see* **ELIZABETH**

LISETTE *see* **ELIZABETH**

LIZ, LIZZY *see* ELIZABETH

LLEWELLYN, LLYWELYN *m.*
(*lóowel'in, hlẹwel'in*)

from Welsh. The meaning is doubtful but is possibly 'like a lion'. It is an old Welsh name which was anglicised into Leolin(e) as early as the 13th century. This form was used at least until the 17th century, when Lewis replaced it. Llewelyn, properly Llywelyn, is one of the commonest Christian names in Wales.

LLOYD *m.* (*loid, hloid*)

a very popular Welsh Christian name, meaning 'grey'. Floyd is a variant form which has arisen owing to the difficulty of pronouncing the Welsh 'Ll'. It is mainly found in North America. A famous example is Floyd Patterson, the former heavyweight boxing champion.

LO, LOLITA *see* DOLORES, LOLA

LOIS *f.* (*lō'is*)

In the New Testament, Lois was the

grandmother of Timothy. As the rest of the family had Greek names, Lois is probably Greek also, but its meaning is not known. Like many obscure Biblical names, it was taken into use in the 17th century by Puritans. It fell out of use but was revived at the beginning of the 20th century.

LOLA *f.* (lō'lẹ)

This was originally a diminutive of the Spanish Dolores (q.v.) and of Carlotta. It has occasionally been used in North America and in Britain, where the name has been given to a famous breed of racing cars. The diminutive Lolita has become well-known in the 20th century through Vladimir Nabokov's novel of that name.

LOLITA *see* LOLA

LORA, LORETTA *see* LAURA

LORNA *f.* (law'nẹ)

This name was created by R. D. Blackmore for the heroine of his novel *Lorna*

Doone. He may have had in mind the Marquis of Lorne or the Old English word meaning 'lost', 'forsaken'. Since the publication of the book in 1869, the name has been quite popular.

LORRAINE *f.* (*lorān'*)

This is the French form of the Old German place name Lotharingen, meaning 'from Lothar's place'. Lothar was an Old German warrior name meaning 'famous army'. Lorraine is a Christian name in France, and has been borrowed with growing frequency in Britain and North America, sometimes in the form Loraine.

LOTTIE, LOTTY *see* CHARLOTTE

LOUIS *see* LEWIS

LOUISA, LOUISE *f.* (*lŏŏēz'ẹ, lŏŏēz'*)

Louise is the French, and Louisa the Latin, feminine form of Louis (q.v.). Though common much earlier in France, Louise did not come to Britain until the 17th century, when Louise de

Kéroual became Charles II's favourite. It was popular for about a century until Louisa superseded it. Today both are about equally common.

LOWIS *see* **LEWIS**

LUCAS *see* **LUKE**

LUCASTA, LUCETTE, LUCILLA *see* **LUCY**

LUCE *see* **LUCY**

LUCIA *see* **LUCY**

LUCIAN *m.* (*lōō′siẹn*)

from Latin Lucianus, but originally a Greek word of obscure meaning. The early historical bearers of the name were from Syria and Asia Minor. Lucianus appears, though rarely, in medieval times, and has occasionally been given since the Renaissance. Since the 19th century, Lucian has been the current form, but it is still rare. A feminine form, Luciana, is sometimes found.

LUCIANA *see* **LUCIAN**

LUCIANUS *see* LUCIAN

LUCILLA, LUCILLE *f.* (*lōōsil'e, lōōsēl'*)

These are feminine diminutives of the Latin Lucius (q.v.). Lucilla was the name of several Roman empresses and of a 3rd century Roman martyr. Lucille is the French form which has recently become generally known in Britain.

LUCINA *see* LUCY

LUCINDA *f.* (*lōōsin'de*)

Originally a poetic form of Lucy (q.v.), this name is now given independently, and has recently become quite popular. The short form Cindy is sometimes used.

LUCIUS *m.* (*lōō'sies*)

This was a Latin first name derived from *lux*, meaning 'light', and there were three early Popes of this name. The name was first used in England during the Renaissance with the revival of classical learning. It has never had the same popularity as its feminine counterpart, Lucy (q.v.).

LUCRETIA *f.* (*lŏŏkrẹ'shē*)

This is a Roman family name derived from the Latin for 'profit' or 'riches'. Its use as a Christian name in Renaissance Europe was due to Lucretia, the wife of Collatinus, who was raped by Tarquin and committed suicide. This incident led to the expulsion of the Tarquins from Rome. Shakespeare's poem *The Rape of Lucrece* spread the use of the name in this form. It was most common in Britain between the 16th and the 18th century but has never quite died out.

LUCY *f.* (*lŏŏ'si*)

Lucy is the usual English form of the Latin Lucia, the feminine form of Lucius, from *lux*, meaning 'light'. In Roman times, the name often signified that the child had been born at dawn; the goddess Lucina was the patroness of childbirth, bringing the children into the light of day. St. Lucy was a

Sicilian martyr who was much beloved in the Middle Ages, and the name became well established after the Norman Conquest, with the alternative form Luce. The Latin Lucia was used from the 17th century but Lucy is the current form, which is very common in Britain. Other diminutives and derivatives are Lucette, Lucinda (q.v.), Lucasta and Lucilla (q.v.).

LUDOVICUS *see* LEWIS

LUELLA *f.* (*looͤel'ĕ*)

probably from the Old English meaning 'famous elf'. Another possible source is a combination of the names Louise and Ella (qq.v.). Today the name is most popular in North America. Louella is an alternative spelling.

LUKE *m.* (*look'*)

from Greek, latinised as Lucas, meaning 'a man of Lucania'. St. Luke the Evangelist is the patron saint of doctors and also of painters, and the name was often given by a craftsman to his son. The name appeared in the 12th century as Lucas but a century later it was well-established in the English form Luke. There has recently been some revival of the name in Britain, probably due to North American influence.

LUTHER m. (lōō'thẹ)

from the Old German meaning 'famous warrior'. The modern use of Luther as a Christian name is entirely due to Martin Luther, the great German religious leader of the Reformation.

LYDIA f. (lid'iẹ)

from the Greek meaning 'a Lydian girl'. Lydia was a district of Asia Minor where the people were famous merchants, and were said to have invented coinage. In the Acts of the Apostles, Lydia was a widow of Philippi, who was converted by St. Paul when he stayed at her house. The name was not used in this country before the 17th century and it has never been common.

LYN(N) *f.* (*lin*)

from the Old English meaning 'water-fall' or 'pool'. The name is still popular in Britain and North America (*see* LINETTE, CAROLYN).

LYON *see* **LEO**

M

MABBOT *see* **MABEL**

MABBS *see* **MABEL**

MABEL, MABELLA *f.* (*mā'bel, mebel'e*)

Mabel is a shortening of Amabel (q.v.), and Mabella is the latinised form. Both were current from the 12th to the 15th century, but were rare thereafter. Mabel was revived in the 19th century and became very common. It has recently suffered another fall from favour. Such surnames as Mabbs, Mabbot and Mappin are derivations. The pet form often used is May.

MADELEINE *see* MADELINE

MADELINE, MAGDALEN(E) *f.*
(*mad'elin, mag'delin, mag'delēn*)

Magdalene, the original form of the name, is Hebrew, and means 'woman of Magdala', a town on the Sea of Galilee which was the birthplace of St. Mary Magdalene. From about the 12th century the name was used in England in the French form Madeline, often abbreviated to Maudlin and Madlin. Magdalen, the Biblical form, was adopted after the Reformation. It was usually pronounced like Maudlin, but, because the meaning of this word developed into the sense of weak and sentimental, this form was replaced by the current Madeline. It shares the short form Madge with Margaret. Another short form is Magda, which has also been given as an independent name.

MADGE *see* MADELINE, MARGARET

MADLIN, MAUDLIN *see* MADELINE

MADOC *m.* (*mad'ek*)

from the Welsh meaning 'fortunate'. This name is most common in Wales. There is some evidence of its use in the West of England in the 11th century, lasting until the 15th century. It is very rarely used outside Wales today, though more common in Britain are the surnames Mad(d)ox and Maddocks.

MAELMOR *see* MILES

MAERWINE *see* MERVYN

MAGDA *see* MADELINE

MAGGIE *see* MARGARET

MAGNUS *m.* (*mag'nes*)

This is the Latin adjective meaning 'great'. The spread of this name was due to the Emperor Charlemagne, Carolus Magnus. Some of his admirers took Magnus for a personal name, and among those that christened their sons after him was St. Olaf of Norway. The name spread from Scandinavia to Shetland and Ireland. From Shetland the name became well established in Scotland. In Ireland it became Manus, hence the common Irish surname Mc-Manus.

MAIRE see **MARY**

MAIRIN see **MAUREEN**

MAISIE see **MARGARET**

MALCOLM m. (mal'kẹm)

from the Gaelic meaning 'follower of St. Columba'. This is a very popular Scottish name, and four kings of Scotland bore it. It was used very occasionally in medieval England, but it is only recently that it has become common. The most famous bearers of the name in this century are Sir Malcolm Campbell, breaker of the world land speed record, and Sir Malcolm Sargent, the orchestral conductor (see COLUM).

MAMIE see **MARY**

MANDY *see* **AMANDA**

MANFRED *m.* (*man'frid*)

from the Old German meaning 'man peace'. The Normans brought the name to England but it does not occur after Domesday Book until Byron's poem *Manfred* caused it to be used once or twice in the 19th century. It is now only rarely found in Britain.

MANNY *see* **EMANUEL**

MANUEL *see* **EMANUEL**

MANUS *see* **MAGNUS**

MAOLMUIRE *see* **MILES**

MAPPIN *see* **MABEL**

MARCIA *f.* (*mà'shẹ, màs'iẹ*)

the feminine form of the Latin Marcius, a Roman clan name. It probably came originally from the name of the god Mars. St. Marcia was an early Christian martyr. The name's popularity in Britain seems to have grown in recent years, possibly developing as a feminine version of Marcus (q.v.). The commonest variant spelling is Marsha.

MARCIUS *see* MARCIA

MARCUS, MARK *m.* (*mɑ'kəs, mɑ̀k*)

from the name of Mars, the Roman god of war, and a well-known Roman family name and personal name. Although the name occurs from the Middle Ages in Britain, it has only recently become common. The Latin form Marcus is the less common of the two. The modern use of the name is due to the Evangelist St. Mark. In the Middle Ages Venetian merchants captured St. Mark's relics from Alexandria and took them back to Venice where they built the magnificent basilica in his honour. The Venetians were also the bankers of Europe at this time and their coinage bore the symbol of St. Mark, a winged lion, and was therefore called a 'mark'. There was a King Mark in Arthurian legend, a villainous character in the story of the lovers *Tristram and Iseult*. Tennyson's *Idylls of the King* may, therefore, have had something to do with the revival of the name in the 19th century. The French forms Marc and Marcel, the latter derived from the Latin diminutive Marcellus, are also used in Britain today. A well-known modern Mark was the American author who used the pen name Mark Twain.

MAREDUDD *see* MEREDITH

MARGARET *f.* (*ma´gerit*)

from Latin *margarita*, derived from the Greek word meaning 'a pearl', although the ultimate origin is thought to be Persian, for 'child of light'. Apparently the Persians believed that pearls were formed when oysters rose from their beds at night to look at the moon, and trapped a drop of dew in their shells, which was transformed into a pearl by the moonbeams. The name first spread into Scotland in the 11th century on account of St. Margaret, wife of Malcolm III. She was of Hungarian extraction, the name having penetrated into Eastern Europe through the in-

fluence of St. Margaret of Antioch, a
3rd century martyr. The name became
very common in medieval England and,
after a decline, regained its enormous
popularity in the 19th century. This
has persisted to the present day. The
most common pet forms are Madge,
Meg and Peg(gy). Maisie and Maggie
are particularly Scottish variants. Other
diminutives sometimes used are the
German and Swedish Greta, French
Margot and Marguérite, and Italian
Rita (*see* MARGERY, MAY).

MARGE, MARGIE *see* MARGERY

MARGERY, MARJORIE *f.* (mà'jeri)

Margerie was originally a pet form of
the French Marguérite, but it became
established as a proper name in England as early as the 12th century. Marjorie is the spelling in Scotland, where
the name was popular from the late
13th century, after Robert Bruce gave
the name to his daughter. She later
founded the Stuart dynasty by marry-

ing Walter the High Steward. Marge and Margie are pet forms.

MARGOT *see* MARGARET

MARGUÉRITE *see* MARGARET, MARGERY

MARIA, MIRIAM, MARIE *see* MARY

MARIAN, MARION *f.* (*mar'iẹn*)

This name was originally a diminutive of the French Marie (*see* MARY), which was early established as an independent name, and was common on both sides of the English Channel in medieval times. Maid Marian is well-known as Robin Hood's sweetheart. Marian was a later form which was extended to Marianne, giving rise to the double name Mary Anne in the 18th century. Mariana is a Spanish equivalent which is sometimes given in England. The word 'marionette' is a derivative of the name.

MARIANNE *see* MARIAN

MARIE *see* MARY

MARIGOLD *f.* (*mar'igōld*)

This name, borrowed from the flower, was adopted with others in the late 19th century, but has never become common.

MARILYN *f.* (*mar'ẹlin*)

This is a diminutive of Mary (q.v.) now used independently. Its popularity was heightened by the film actress Marilyn Monroe.

MARINA *f.* (*mẹrē'nẹ*)

from Latin *marinus*, meaning 'of the sea'. The name has been used occasionally from at least the 14th century, probably on account of St. Marina of Alexandria, a martyr of the Greek church. The name became more popular in Britain in 1934, when Prince George married Princess Marina of Greece, who later became Duchess of Kent.

MARIO *see* **MARIUS**

MARIOT *see* **MARY**

MARIUS *m.* (*măr′iĕs*)

from a Roman family name, which was first adopted for use during the Renaissance. It has never been common in this country, although Mario is very popular in Italy. The name is probably a derivative of Mars, the Roman god of war and thunder.

MARJORIE *see* **MARGERY**

MARK *see* **MARCUS**

MARMADUC, MARMADUCUS *see* **MARMADUKE**

MARMADUKE *m.* (*mă′mĕdūk*)

from the Irish meaning 'servant of Madoc'. The influence of the Normans on the English language after the Conquest, gave rise to the medieval spelling Marmaduc. The name is practically confined to Yorkshire, which was probably an outpost of Celtic civilization in the North of England. Duke is sometimes used as an abbreviation in the North, but in North America its use is usually derived purely from the title, and Earl, Count and King are also found.

MARSHA *see* MARCIA

MARTELLA, MARTY *see* MARTHA

MARTHA *f.* (mä'thə)

from the Aramaic meaning 'lady'. In the New Testament Martha was the sister of Lazarus and Mary Magdalene. She is described as having been a good and careful housewife. The name was common in France in the Middle Ages, where there was a legend that Martha had travelled to France after the Crucifixion. It was not adopted in Britain until after the Reformation. The name became fairly common, possibly aided to some extent by Flotow's opera *Martha*, which was very popular in the mid 19th century. Variants include Martita and Martella. Marty is the commonest pet form.

MARTIN *m.* (*mǎ'tin*)

from Latin Martinus, a diminutive of Martius, meaning 'of Mars'. Mars was the Roman god of thunder and war. According to popular legend, St. Martin was a 4th century soldier who cut his cloak in two to give half to a beggar one winter's night. He later became Bishop of Tours in France. He also gave his name to two birds, the martin and the martlet. This was the name of five popes, and also of Martin Luther, the great Protestant reformer, so it has been very popular in both churches. It has been used more or less without a break since the 12th century and today is more popular than ever. Martina and Martita, the latter shared with Martha (q.v.), are rare feminine forms.

MARTINA, MARTITA *see* **MARTIN, MARTHA**

MARTINUS, MARTIUS *see* **MARTIN**

MARVIN *see* **MERVYN**

MARY *f.* (*mer'i*)

from Hebrew, probably meaning 'wished-for child'. The earliest form of the name was Miriam (q.v.) and later translations of the Bible changed this to Mariam and Maria, and finally Mary. The name was held to be too sacred for general use until about the 12th century. The French form Marie, and the diminutives Marion and Mariot, were all common. The name was very popular in England until the time of Mary I, 'Bloody Mary', and then Mary Queen of Scots, after which it became unfashionable in some circles. The name did not entirely recover until the mid 17th century. The Scots retained the French Marie, and Maire was the Irish form. The latinised Maria was adopted in the 18th century. Pet forms of Mary were Molly, Polly, Minnie, Mamie and May (*see* MARIAN, MARILYN, MAUREEN, MIRIAM, MOIRA).

MATHEU *see* **MATTHEW**

MATILDA *f.* (m̧etil′ḑe)

from the Old German meaning 'mighty battlemaid'. This name was particularly popular in medieval Court circles, and was introduced by William the Conqueror's wife who bore the name. Later their granddaughter, sometimes known as Maud (q.v.), fought to oust her cousin Stephen from the throne. The name fell into disuse but returned to favour in the 18th century. Tilly is the pet form. Matilda is best known today in the popular Australian song *Waltzing Matilda.*

MATT *see* **MATTHEW**

MATTHAEUS *see* **MATTHEW**

MATTHEW, MATTHIAS *m.* (math′ū, m̧ethī′̧es)

from Hebrew meaning 'gift of God', and the name of one of the Evangelists. In England the name first appears in Domesday Book, in the Latin form Matthaeus and the French Matheu, from which the usual English form

Matthew is derived. The name was particularly popular from the 12th to the 14th centuries. After the Reformation Matthias was adopted, the name of the apostle chosen to succeed Judas Iscariot. Today the English form is fairly common, and the usual short form is Matt.

MAUD(E) f. (mawd)

from the Old French form of the name Matilda (q.v.). This name was popular in Britain after the Norman Conquest, but fell out of use about the 15th century. It was revived in the 19th century by Tennyson's well-known poem *Maud*. Maudie is sometimes used as a pet form.

MAUDIE see MAUD

MAURA see MOIRA

MAUREEN f. (maw'rēn)

from the Irish Máirín, a diminutive of Máire (*see* MARY). The fashion for Maureen has probably come to England from North America. Another possible derivation is the Old French word meaning 'a Moor', which was the feminine form of Maurice (q.v.). The variant forms in Britain are Moreen and Moira (q.v.).

MAURICE, MORRIS *m.* (*mor'is*)

from the Latin Mauritius meaning 'a Moor'. The spread of the name was due to St. Maurice, a 3rd century martyr in Switzerland, after whom the town of St. Moritz was named. The Normans brought the name to England as Meurisse, which was soon anglicised to Morris. A 'morris dance' is really a 'moorish dance'. The more modern French Maurice has now to a large extent replaced the English form, although it is pronounced the same way. In Ireland it has been used to translate the native Moriarty. There is a very old Welsh equivalent Meurig which occurs in the 5th century. Short forms are Morrie and Maurie.

MAVIS *f.* (*mā'vis*)

This is an old name derived from the

French word for a song-thrush. It was first used as a Christian name by Marie Corelli in 1895 in her novel *The Sorrows of Satan*, for a character called Mavis Clare. Since then it has become fairly common in this country.

MAX *see* MAXIMILIAN

MAXIMILIAN *m.* (*maximil'iẹn*)

Maximus in Latin means 'greatest'. Two 3rd century saints bore the name Maximilian, but despite this, it is popularly thought to have been invented by the German Emperor Frederick III, combining the last names of Quintus Fabius Maximus, and Scipio Aemilianus, two great Roman generals. His son, later Emperor Maximilian I, was a reckless huntsman and fighter, and his name became very popular throughout Austria and the German speaking peoples. The name has occasionally been used in England, mainly by people of German extraction like Sir Max Beerbohm, author and caricaturist. Max is the usual abbreviation.

MAXIMUS *see* **MAXIMILIAN**

MAXINE *f.* (*max'ēn*)

This is a modern French diminutive of Max (*see* MAXIMILIAN), which has been used in England and North America as a feminine name.

MAXWELL *m.* (*maks'wel*)

from Old English, probably meaning 'great' and 'spring'. Though mainly a surname, it has been given as a Christian name in the last hundred years.

MAY *f.* (*mā*)

This was originally a pet form of Margaret or Mary (qq.v.) but it has more recently been associated with the month (c.f. June, April), and it is now a separate name. Film actresses Mae West and Mai Britt have made these variant spellings familiar.

MEG *see* **MARGARET**

MELANIA *see* **MELANIE**

MELANIE, MELLONEY *f.* (mel'<i>e</i>ni)

from the Greek meaning 'black' or 'dark-skinned'. Melania is an ancient name known to both the Greeks and the Romans. The name came to England from France in the mid-17th century in the French form Mélanie, which became Melloney and Melanie in Britain. It was particularly popular in the West of England. The Latin Melania was used occasionally in the 19th century, but all forms are now rare.

MELISENDA, MELISENT
see MILLICENT

MELISSA *f.* (melis'<i>e</i>)

from the Greek meaning 'a bee'. This is the name of a nymph, and also the legendary woman, murdered by her husband Periander, ruler of Corinth, who wandered naked in the underworld, because her funeral clothes had not been ceremonially burned. It was used occasionally in the 18th century but is now practically obsolete.

MELLONEY *see* MELANIE

MELVIN, MELVYN *m.* (*melvin*)

probably from the Irish meaning 'polished chief', a description of the knight's sword. It has also been traced from Old English Maelwine, meaning 'sword friend' or 'speech friend'.

MEREDITH *m.* (*mer'edith*)

from the Welsh Maredudd, meaning 'great chief'. Alternative meanings that have been suggested are, 'mortal day' and 'guardian from the sea.' As a Christian name it is exclusively Welsh, but as a surname it is more widespread. It is sometimes spelt Meridith.

MERLE *f.* (*mēl*)

This is the French for 'blackbird' originally derived from Latin. It was adopted as a Christian name in the 19th century. It is well-known as the name of the American film actress Merle Oberon, and there is a Madame

Merle in Henry James' novel *Portrait of a Lady*. The name is rather rare today.

MERLIN *m.* (*mę'lin*)

from the Welsh Myrddin, possibly meaning 'sea hill'. It was the name of a legendary poet and prophet of the 6th century, and of the magician in Arthurian legends. It is not often found.

MERVYN *m.* (*me'vin*)

There are two possible etymologies for this very old name. There was an Anglo-Saxon name Maerwine, meaning 'famous friend' from which Marvin was derived. Better known is Myrddin, Welsh 'sea-hill', which is the true form of Merlin, King Arthur's legendary magician. Mervyn is best known in Britain today for Dr. Mervyn Stockwood, Bishop of Southwark. Marvin is more common as a surname.

MEURIG *see* **MAURICE**

MEURISSE *see* **MAURICE**

MICAH *see* **MICHAEL**

MICHAEL m. (mīk'el)

from the Hebrew meaning 'who is
like the Lord?' In the Bible Michael
was one of the seven archangels, and
their leader in battle, and therefore the
patron of soldiers. The name was common from the 12th century but the
spelling and pronunciation varied con-
siderably, Machel, Mihiel and Mighel
being the most common. The variant
form Micah, the name of a minor
prophet in the Old Testament, was
used in the 17th century among Puritans.
Michael is now common throughout
Britain and has pet forms Mike, Mick,
Micky. Sometimes shortened to Miles.

MICHEL, MIGHEL, MIHIEL
see MICHAEL

MICK, MIKE *see* MICHAEL

MILBURGA *see* MILDRED

MILDGYTH *see* MILDRED
MILDRED f. (mil'drid)

The 7th century King Merowald of the

Old English Kingdom of Mercia had three daughters; Milburga, 'gentle defence', Mildgyth, 'gentle gift', and Mildthryth, 'gentle strength'. It was from the last of these that Mildred was derived and the popularity of the three sisters, all of whom were canonised, led to the name becoming common in the Middle Ages. It was revived in the 19th century.

MILDTHRYTH *see* MILDRED

MILES m. (*mīls*)

probably from one of the compounds of the Old German root, *mil* meaning, 'beloved'. Another possible derivation is the Latin for 'soldier'. The Normans brought to Britain the forms Miles, Milo and Milon. Miles was quite a popular name in the Middle Ages and it survived as a surname until its revival as a Christian name in the 19th century. This revival may have been partly due to the use of the name in Ireland to transliterate the Irish Maolmuire and Maelmor. The name is sometimes used as a reduction of Michael. A variant spelling is Myles.

MILLICENT, MELICENT *f.* *(mil'isent, mel'isent)*

from the Old German meaning 'strong worker'. This name was common in France about a thousand years ago, when it had the form Melisenda. The French brought it to England in the late 12th century in the form Melisent, and it survived with minor changes of spelling well into the 17th century. In the 19th and 20th centuries it has been revived, and Millicent is the most common form, with Milly as a common abbreviation.

MILLY *see* **EMILY, MILLICENT**

MILO, MILON *see* **MILES**

MINN *see* **MIRIAM**

MINNA, MINNIE *see* **MARY, MIRIAM WILHELMINA**

MIRA *see* **MYRA**

MIRABEL, MIRABELLE *f.* (*mir′abel*)

from Latin meaning 'wonderful'. The Latin form Mirabella was used in the 12th century, but it was later anglicised as Mirabel. It was rare until the 19th century, but is now found fairly often.

MIRANDA *f.* (*miran′də*)

from Latin meaning 'to be admired'. This name was first used by Shakespeare for the heroine of *The Tempest*, a young girl blessed with many admirable qualities. Like other unusual Shakespearian names it has been used quite frequently in the 20th century.

MIRIAM *f.* (*mir′iəm*)

from Hebrew, probably meaning 'wished-for child'. This is the oldest known form of Mary (q.v.) and, in the book of Exodus in the Old Testament, it was the name of the sister of Moses and Aaron. It first became common in Britain in the 17th century and is especially popular among Jews. Short forms which are sometimes found in connection with this name are Minn, Minnie and Mitzi.

MITZI *see* **MIRIAM**

MODESTY *f.* (*mod'esti*)

This abstract virtue name has been used occasionally since the Puritans first adopted it, with many others, in the 17th century. It is perhaps best known for the heroine of popular fiction *Modesty Blaise*.

MOIRA *f.* (*moi're*)

an English rendering of the Irish Maire and Moire, Irish forms of Mary (q.v.). The name has spread to Britain and America where it has flourished. Maura and Maureen (q.v.) have the same origin, but have developed quite independently as separate names, though Moira is very occasionally used as a short form of Maureen.

MOIRE *see* **MOIRA**

MOLLY *see* **MARY**

MONA *f.* (*mō'nę*)

This name is derived from a diminutive of Irish *muadh*, meaning 'noble'. It came into use in the late 19th century along with other Irish names which spread throughout Britain at that time, during a general revival of interest in the Celtic race.

MONICA *f.* (*mon'ikę*)

The etymology of this name is uncertain, but it could be connected with Greek *monos* meaning 'alone' or Latin *moneo*, meaning 'to advise.' St. Monica was the mother of St. Augustine and was a paragon of motherly and wifely virtues. The name has become particularly popular in the 20th century. Mona is sometimes used as a short form.

MONTAGU(E) *m.* (*mon'tęgū*)

The founder of this ancient and noble family was Drogo de Montacute, a companion of William the Conqueror, who was granted estates in Somerset. He took his name from Mont Aigu, a 'pointed hill' in Normandy. The use of Montagu(e) as a Christian name dates from the 19th century, when many aristocratic surnames were adopted by the general public, e.g. Cecil, Howard, Dudley, Mortimer, Percy.

MONTGOMERY *m.* (*montgom'ĕri*)

from the Old French meaning 'mountain of the rich one.' Though mainly a surname, it has occasionally been used as a Christian name in the last hundred years.

MORAG *f.* (*mo'rag*)

from Gaelic, a diminutive of *mor(a)* meaning 'great'. Another possibility is that the name is a variant of Mary. In Gaelic it is used as an equivalent of Sarah (q.v.).

MORAY *see* MURRAY

MORCANT *see* MORGAN

MOREEN *see* MAUREEN

MORGAN *m. and f.* (*maw'gen*)

In its earliest form, Morcant, this name meant 'seabright', but it later absorbed another name, Morien, meaning 'seaborn'. Its earliest celebrated bearer was the first recorded British heretic, who was known as Pelagius, a Greek rendering of the name. Today Morgan is a favourite Welsh Christian name and surname.

MORIARTY *see* MAURICE

MORIEN *see* MORGAN

MORITZ *see* MAURICE

MORNA, MYRNA *f.* (*maw'ne, me'ne*)

Both these names come from the Irish name Muirne, which means 'beloved' or 'gentle'. Both have recently become common in other parts of Britain.

MORRIE, MAURIE *see* MAURICE

MORRIS *see* MAURICE

MORRISON *m.* (*mor'ison*)

from the Scottish clan name. Like many

other surnames, it is now used occasionally as a Christian name, mainly among Scots.

MORTIMER m. (maw'timę)

an aristocratic surname generally adopted as a Christian name in the 19th century. The surname was derived from the French word Mortemer, meaning 'dead sea'. The Mortimer family connect it with the Dead Sea in Palestine, where their ancestors fought in crusading times. The pet form Morty was also used independently in Ireland as a transliteration of the Irish name Murtagh. This was then lengthened to Mortimer, and in this way the name became established. The short form Mort is also used.

MORTY see MORTIMER

MORVEN m. and f. (maw'vęn)

from the Irish meaning 'tall blonde one'. It is a predominantly Irish name.

MORWENNA *f.* (*maw'wene̜*)

from Welsh, probably meaning 'sea-wave'. There was a saint of this name about whom little is known, and the name is confined to Wales and the West Country.

MOSES *m.* (*mō'ziz*)

The meaning of this name is uncertain and it is possibly Egyptian, rather than Hebrew. It became common among Jews after their return from captivity in Babylon. In Britain it first appears in Domesday Book as Moyses, which became Moyse or Moss in general use. The present form, Moses, which was not used until after the Reformation, is the form used in the Authorised Version of the Bible.

MOSS *see* **MOSES**

MOYSE, MOYSES *see* **MOSES**

MUIR *m.* (*mūer'*)

This is a Scottish surname meaning 'moor', and sometimes spelt Mure. It is occasionally used as a Christian name among Scots. A famous example is Muir Mathieson, the conductor.

MUIRGHEAL *see* MURIEL

MUNGO *m.* (mung'gō)

This name was originally a term of affection given to St. Kentigern by his followers, and, in Gaelic, it means 'beloved'. He was a 6th century bishop of Glasgow and is generally known as St. Mungo. The name is confined to Scotland, and the most famous bearer was Mungo Park, the 18th century explorer who wrote *Travels in the Interior of Africa*, a very well-known book about his voyage down the river Niger.

MURDOCH *m.* (me̗'dō)

This popular Scottish name is derived from the Gaelic meaning 'seaman', and is equivalent to the Irish Murtagh (*see* MORTIMER). It is also quite common as a surname when it is pronounced me̗'doH.

MURIEL, MERIEL *f.* (*mūr′iĕl, mer′iĕl*)

from the Irish Muirgheal, meaning 'seabright'. The name came to England at the time of the Norman Conquest, through the many Celts who were settled in Brittany and Normandy, and came to Britain with William the Conqueror. Both forms were in common use until the mid-14th century. Muriel was revived in the 19th century and Meriel has recently come back into use also. Muriel Spark is a well-known novelist.

MURRAY *m.* (*mur′i*)

from the Gaelic meaning 'sea'. The Scottish clan of Murray, or Moray, probably took its name from the Moray Firth in the North East of Scotland. James Stuart, Earl of Moray, was half-brother of Mary Queen of Scots, and he acted as Regent when she was imprisoned in Loch Leven Castle. His fame gave rise to the use of Moray as a Christian name in Scotland, but today the form Murray is more common.

MURTAGH see **MORTIMER**

MYFANWY f. (mifan'wi)

a well-known Welsh name meaning
'my rare one'. The commonest short
forms in Wales are Fanny and Myfi.

MYLES see **MILES**

MYRA f. (mī're)

This name appears to have been invented in the 16th century by Lord
Brooke for the object of his love poems,
and until the 19th century, it was used
exclusively by poets and novelists. The
most celebrated bearer of the name was
Dame Myra Hess the pianist. The variant
form Mira is also found, but usually as a
short form of Mirabel or Miranda.
(qq.v.).

MYRDDIN see **MERLIN, MERVYN**

MYRNA see **MORNA**

MYRTILL see **MYRTLE**

MYRTLE f. (me'tl)

One of the flower names, in this case a

shrub, which, since the 19th century, has been used as a girl's name. The name is Greek, and in Ancient Greece the Myrtle was a symbol of victory. The variant form, Myrtilla, is also occasionally found.

N

NAB *see* **ABEL**

NADINE *f.* (*na'dēn*)

This is a French name which is derived from the Russian word for 'hope'. It is occasionally found in Britain, but only since the 20th century. The variant forms Nada and Nadia are also current. Nadia Nerina is a well-known British ballerina.

NAN, NANNY *see* **ANN**

NANCY, NAN(NY) *see* **ANN**

NAOMI *f.* (*nā'ōmi*)

from the Hebrew meaning 'pleasant'. In the Old Testament Naomi was the mother-in-law of Ruth, whose two sons died in Moab. The name was adopted with many other Old Testament names by the Puritans in the 17th century. It is well-known among Jews, and is still a fairly popular name.

NAT *see* NATHAN, NATHANIEL

NATALIE, NATALIA *f.* (*nat'ęli, natàl'ię*)

from the Latin *natale domini*, meaning 'the birthday of the Lord'. Natalia and its diminutive, Natasha, are popular names in Russia. The French form Natalie is quite common on the Continent, but is also found occasionally in Britain. Natalie Wood is a well-known modern film actress. The short form Nelly is sometimes used.

NATASHA *see* NATALIE

NATHAN *m.* (*nă'thęn*)

from the Hebrew meaning 'gift'. It is best known for the prophet in the Old Testament who condemned King David for putting Uriah in the front line of battle, so that he might be killed, and David could marry his widow, Bathsheba. It has been used occasionally since the 17th century, but is more common in North America than in Britain today. Nathan Milstein is a well-known violinist. The name shares the short form, Nat, with Nathaniel.

NATHANIEL m. (nẹthan'iẹl)

from the Hebrew meaning 'gift of God'. It was the Christian name of the apostle who was better known as Bartholomew. The name was rare in Britain until after Shakespeare's use of it in *Love's Labour Lost*. This made the name better known, but it is more common in North America today than in Britain. Nathaniel Hawthorne is a famous American novelist of the 19th century. Nat is the short form.

NEAL, NEIL *see* **NIGEL**

NED *see* **EDWARD**

NEL, NEEL, NELE *see* **NIGEL**

NELL *see* **ELEANOR**

NELL(Y) *f. (nel, nel'i)*

the pet form of Ellen, Helen and Eleanor (qq.v.). It was already in use in Britain in the Middle Ages, and a famous holder of the name was Nell (Eleanor) Gwyn, mistress of Charles II. The name is still fairly popular in Britain.

NESSA, NESSIE *see* **AGNES**

NEST, NESTA *see* **AGNES**

NET, NETTIE *see* **ANTONY**

NETTA, NETTIE *see* **JANET**

NETTY *see* **NATALIE**

NEVILLE *m. (nev'el)*

from the French surname Neuville, meaning 'new town'. It was introduced into England at the time of the Norman Conquest, when the Neville family, who came over with William the Conqueror, were very powerful. Their influence continued , but the name was not adopted as a Christian name until the 17th century. Famous holders of the name were Neville Chamberlain, Prime Minister of Britain at the outbreak of the Second World War, and Nevil Shute the novelist. The latter shows a variant spelling.

NIALL *see* NIGEL

NICHOLAS *m.* (*nik'ōlĕs*)

from the Greek meaning 'victory of the people'. The name was very popular in the Middle Ages as a result of the influence of St. Nicholas, who was the patron of children and sailors. The usual forms then were Nicol, and in Latin Nicholaus. The use of Claus in 'Santa Claus' is taken from the modern corruption of the German form Klaus. The name faded out at the time of the Reformation, but it is now one of the most popular Christian names in Britain. Nick and Nicky are the pet forms

NICHOLAUS *see* NICHOLAS

NICK, NICKY *see* NICHOLAS

NICOL *see* NICHOLAS

NICOLA, NICOLETTE *f.* (*nik′ōlẹ, nikōlet′*)

These are respectively the Italian and French feminine forms of Nicholas (q.v.). Nicola was used as early as the reign of King John, when Nicola de Camville resisted the French attack on Lincoln. In modern times Nicole and Nicolette have become quite common in Britain. Colette may have increased in popularity due to the French writer of this name.

NICOLE *see* **COLETTE, NICOLA**

NIGEL, NIALL, NEAL, NEIL *m.* (*nī′jẹl, nēl′*)

The origin of this name has been separately traced back to the Irish word *niadh*, meaning 'champion', and the Icelandic hero's name Njal. The Normans first brought the name to England as Nel, Neel, Nele. This was latinised as Nigellus, which was later thought to be a diminutive from *niger* meaning 'black', and the forms Nigell, Nygell, and eventually Nigel, became popular names in the Middle Ages. Various forms of Niall continued in use. Neil and Nigel are common mostly in Scotland while Niall is common in Ireland, and Neal in England.

NIGELL, NIGELLUS *see* **NIGEL**

NINIAN *m.* (*nin'ien*)

the name of a 5th century saint who converted the Picts in the South of Scotland to Christianity. It is now found mostly in Scotland and, occasionally, in the North of England.

NITA *see* **JOANNA**

NOEL *m. and f.* (*nō'el*)

This is an old French name derived from *dies natalis*, meaning 'birthday'. The name refers to Christmas Day, and was often given to children born on that day. Nowell is an English spelling which is also used and Noelle is an alternative feminine form.

NOELLE *see* **NOEL**

NORA(H) *f.* (*naw'rę*)

an Irish abbreviation of Honora (q.v.), now used as a separate name. It is also found as a short form for Elinor and Leonora (qq.v.). In Ireland the pet form Noreen is used.

NORMA *f.* (*naw'mę*)

possibly from the Latin meaning 'rule' or 'precept'. The name was known in the 13th century, but was not generally used in Britain until the great success of Bellini's opera *Norma*, in the 19th century, brought the name into popular favour. It is still a fairly common name. Norma Shearer is a well-known film actress. The name has been used as a feminine counterpart of Norman (q.v.).

NORMAN *m.* (*naw'men*)

from the Old English meaning 'from the north'. It was used in Britain before the Norman Conquest, and was popular until the 14th century. It has long been common in Scotland, and for a while was considered a purely Scottish name,

being used as a substitute for the Gaelic
Tormod. It is common throughout
Britain today.

NORRIS m. (nor′is)

from the French meaning 'Northerner'.
It was originally used to describe the
Vikings, and became known in Britain
after the Norman Conquest. It is not
common in the 20th century.

NOWELL see NOEL

NYE see ANEURIN

NYGELL see NIGEL

O

OBADIAH m. (ōbĕdī′e̦)

from the Hebrew meaning 'serving
the Lord' and the name of an Old
Testament Hebrew prophet. It became
fairly common in the 17th century
when the Puritans adopted many of
these less well-known Bible names. It
fell out of favour in the 19th century.

OBERON *see* **AUBREY**

OCTAVIUS *m.* (oktā'vięs)

from a Roman family or clan name, derived from the Latin meaning 'eighth'. It is used as a given name for an eighth child, and is much rarer today than it was in the 19th century.

ODETTE *see* **OTTILIE**

ODYSSEUS *see* **ULYSSES**

OLAF *see* **OLIVER**

OLGA *f.* (ol'gę)

from the Norse word *helga*, meaning 'holy'. The founder of the Russian monarchy is supposed to have been a Scandinavian traveller, and it was in Russia that Olga evolved. Helga is used in Scandinavia. St. Olga was the wife of the Duke of Kiev in the 10th century, and she helped spread Christianity in Russia. Olga came to England with other Russian names in the 19th century, but has not been popular.

OLIVE, OLIVIA *f.* (*ol'iv, oliv'ię*)

from the Latin *oliva*, meaning 'olive'.
St. Oliva was venerated as the protectress
of the olive crops in Italy. The name
was first found in England in the early
13th century. Shakespeare used Olivia
in *Twelfth Night*, giving it some contemporary vogue and a revival in the
18th and 19th centuries. It was used again
in the 18th century by Goldsmith in
The Vicar of Wakefield. Both forms are
still used occasionally.

OLIVER *m.* (*ol'ivę*)

The modern use of this name is derived
from the French for an olive tree. It
was the name of one of the most famous
of Charlemagne's peers. However, the
name may go back further and be connected with the Norse Olaf. Oliver was
popular until the parliamentary revolu-
tion led by Oliver Cromwell in the 17th
century, after which the name fell out
of favour. It was revived in the 19th
century and became quite common.

OLWEN, OLWYN *f.* (*ol'win*)

from the Welsh meaning 'white foot-print'. This name first occurs in the old Celtic legend in which Olwen, a giant's daughter, is wooed by a prince, who has to enlist the aid of King Arthur to accomplish the tasks that are set him. She was named Olwen because 'white trefoils sprang up wherever she trod'. The name became very popular in Wales, and spread to England in 1849 when a new translation of the *Mabinogion*, a collection of Celtic legends, was published.

ONUPHRIOS *see* HUMPHREY

OONA, OONAGH *see* UNA

OPHELIA *f.* (*ōfē'lie*)

from the Greek meaning 'help'. It appears to have been adopted by an early 16th century writer, but its modern use is largely due to the fame of Shakespeare's play *Hamlet*. In the play, Ophelia is the girl who loves Hamlet and who eventually goes mad and is drowned.

ORIANA *f. (orið'nę)*

from the Latin for 'dawn'. This name is first recorded in the 16th century, when madrigal writers used it as a name for Queen Elizabeth I. The name was revived in the 19th century, and Tennyson wrote a poem called *The Ballad of Oriana*. It is rarely used today.

ORLANDO *m. (awlan'dō)*

This is the Italian form of Roland (q.v.). Italian names were fashionable in the 16th century, and Shakespeare used this one in his play *As You Like It*. It was the name of a very well-known 20th century novel by Virginia Woolf, and it is still found occasionally.

ORSON *m. (aw'sęn)*

from Old French Ourson, meaning 'little bear'. This is not a common name, though it is familiar through Orson Welles, the American actor and director.

ORTENSIA *see* HORTENSIA

ORVILLE *m.* (*aw'vil*)

from Old French meaning 'golden town'. It is a fairly rare name in Britain. A famous example was Orville Wright, the aviation pioneer.

OSBERT *m.* (*oz'bet*)

from Old English meaning 'godbright'. It was mainly used in Northumbria in the Anglo-Saxon period, and was reinforced at the time of the Norman Conquest by the Norman Osbert, of Old German origin. It survived until the 19th century, when it became quite popular. The best known modern example in Britain is Osbert Lancaster, the cartoonist and satirist.

OSCAR *m.* (*os'ke*)

from the Old English Osgar, meaning 'godspear'. It was in use before the Norman Conquest, but seems to have died out soon after. James Macpherson gave the name to Ossian's son in his poems, and Napoleon's enthusiasm for the Ossianic legend caused him to give the name Oscar to his godson, later King of Sweden. It became widespread on the Continent and in the last hundred years it has been regularly used in England and Ireland. The scandal with which the author and playwright Oscar Wilde was associated in the 19th century, caused it to fall from favour.

OSGAR *see* OSCAR

OSWALD *m.* (*oz'wĕld*)

from the Old English meaning 'god power'. Oswald, King of Northumbria in the 7th century, was killed fighting the Welsh at Oswestry. He was later canonized, and the place took its name from him. A second St. Oswald helped St. Dunstan with his church reforms in the 10th century. Because of these two saints, the name was popular in the Middle Ages and has never entirely died out.

OTTILIE *f.* (*ot'ili*)

This is the usual modern form of Ottilia, which is derived from the Old German

meaning 'girl (or woman) of the father-
land'. St. Ottilie is the patron saint of
Alsace. The French form Odette has
also been used occasionally in Britain.

OWEN *m.* (ō′win)

This is one of the most popular of all
Welsh names, but its origin is uncertain.
It may have come from Latin Eugenius
meaning 'well-born', or Welsh *oen*,
meaning 'lamb'. It may also be the
same as Ewen (q.v.), and hence mean
'a youth'. There are many bearers of
the name in Welsh history and legend,
but the best known is Owen Glendower,
who fought for Welsh independence in
the 15th century. The name has spread
to the rest of Britain and to North
America.

P

PADDY, PAT *see* **PATRICK,
PATRICIA**

PAM *see* **PAMELA**

PAMELA *f.* (*pam'ele*)

from the Greek meaning 'all honey'. This name dates only from the late 16th century when it was coined by Sir Philip Sydney for his romance *Arcadia*. It did not come into general use until the 18th century when Samuel Richardson's novel *Pamela* was popular. It has been most used in the 20th century, and Pam is the usual pet form. The original pronunciation, which is no longer used, was *pamē'le*.

PAT *see* **PATRICIA, PATRICK**

PAT, PATTY *see* **PATRICIA**

PATIENCE *f.* (*pā'shens*)

This name was fashionable in the 17th century when girls were named after abstract virtues. It is on record that Sir Thomas Carew called his four daughters, Patience, Temperance, Silence and Prudence. It dropped out of popular use in the 19th century, but it is still occasionally found.

PATRICIA *f.* (*pĕtrish'ḛ*)

the feminine of Latin *patricius*, meaning
'nobleman.' It was originally only used
in Latin records to distinguish a bearer
of the name Patrick who was female, but
it was used independently from the 18th
century. It has become common only in
the last hundred years, owing to the
popularity of Queen Victoria's granddaughter Princess Patricia of Connaught.
Current abbreviations are Pat, Patty,
Paddy and Tricia (*trish'ḛ*). (*see* PATRICK).

PATRICK *m.* (*pat'rik*)

from the Latin meaning 'nobleman'.
St. Patrick adopted this name at his
ordination. He was born in Scotland
but was captured by pirates when still
a boy and sold as a slave in Ireland.
Although he escaped, he wished to
convert the Irish to Christianity, so,
after training as a missionary in France,
he returned to devote his life to this
cause. The Irish thought his name too
sacred for use until about the 17th
century, and it became common first

in Scotland in the Middle Ages, whence it spread to the North of England. In Scotland Peter and Patrick were interchangeable right up to the late 19th century. Pat and Paddy are short forms, the latter being used as a generic term for an Irishman.

PAUL m. (pawl)

from the Latin meaning 'small'. The New Testament tells how Saul of Tarsus adopted this name after his conversion. The name was not common until the 17th century. It was often coupled with the name Peter, as the saints Peter and Paul share a feast day. A notable example of this was Sir Peter Paul Rubens, the 17th century painter. Paul became more popular after the Reformation, Peter having fallen into disfavour. Paul Jones was a Scottish Admiral who served in the American navy during the American War of Independence, and there is a popular dance named after him. The name does not occur much in English literature, but it is fairly common today.

PAULA, PAULINA, PAULINE *f.*
(*paw'lẹ, pawlē'nẹ, paw'lēn*)

These are feminine derivatives of the
Latin for 'small'. There was a 4th
century St. Paula who founded several
convents in Bethlehem, and thus gave
the name some vogue in the Middle
Ages. Paulina and Pauline are respectively the Latin and French forms.
The latter has been more often used
in modern times, though there are
signs that Paula is superseding it.
Polly is sometimes used as a pet form.

PAULINUS *m.* (*pawlē'nẹs*)

a derivative of the Latin for 'small'.
St. Paulinus was a missionary sent to
Britain by St. Gregory in the 7th century, and the name has a long history
of use in Britain, though it has never
been common.

PEARL *f.* (*pẹl*)

This name first became common in the
19th century, with other gem names (*see*
BERYL, RUBY). It has also been used as a

pet name for Margaret (q.v.), which is derived from the Greek for 'pearl'. There is a 14th century Middle English poem about a little girl called Pearl, where the name is probably allegorical. In America it has occasionally been used as a man's name.

PEG, PEGGY *see* **MARGARET**

PEN, PENNY *see* **PENELOPE**

PENELOPE *f.* (pĕnel'ōpi)

from Greek. The first element may be *pene*, meaning 'bobbin'. In Homer's *Odyssey*, it was the name of Odysseus' wife, who waited ten years for her husband to return from the Trojan War. The name has been used regularly, though infrequently, since the 16th century. It has been more popular in Ireland where it is used as an equivalent of the native Fenella (q.v.). It is often abbreviated to Pen or Penny.

PEPPI *see* **PERPETUA**

PERCE *see* **PERCEVAL, PERCY**

PERCEVAL, PERCIVAL *m.* (*pe͞' sivel*)

The origin of this name is obscure. It has been suggested that it is a combination of French *perce* and *val*, meaning 'pierce valley'. When used as a surname, Perceval probably referred to Percheval, a place in Normandy. The name has been used in this country since the 14th century but is not common. The short form is Perce (*see* PERCY).

PERCY *m.* (*pe͞' si*)

This famous northern family is descended from William de Perci, one of William the Conqueror's companions, who took his name from a village in Normandy (*see* PERCEVAL). At first its use as a Christian name was confined to connections of the Percy family, but during the 19th century it came into general use, probably partly due to the poet, Percy Bysshe Shelley. It shares the short form Perce with Perceval.

PERDITA *f.* (*pe'dite*)

This is the feminine of Latin *perditus*, meaning 'lost'. It was coined by Shakespeare for the heroine of *A Winter's Tale*. It has been used very occasionally since, as a direct result of this.

PEREGRINE *m.* (*per'egrin*)

from Latin *peregrinus*, meaning 'stranger' or 'traveller' and hence 'pilgrim'. There was a 7th century saint of this name who was a hermit near Modena. The name has been used in this country since about the 13th century, but it has always been rare.

PERPETUA *f.* (*pepet'ūe*)

from the Latin meaning 'everlasting' or 'perpetual'. The name is used mostly by Roman Catholics in commemoration of a 3rd century Christian martyr. A diminutive is Peppi.

PERRY *m.* (*per'i*)

This name sometimes occurs as an abbreviation of Peregrine (q.v.) but it may also have an independent origin from the Middle English Pereye, which is derived from the French meaning 'Little Peter' (*see* PETER).

PETE *see* PETER

PETER *m.* (*pē'ter*)

from the Greek for 'rock'. Cephas is the Aramaic equivalent which Jesus gave as a nickname to Simon bar Jonah, to be symbolic of steadfastness in faith. Peter was chief of the Apostles and became the first Bishop of Rome. He was the favourite saint of the medieval church and his name was very popular throughout Christendom in the Middle Ages. In England the name is first recorded in Domesday Book in the Latin form Petrus. The Normans brought over the French form Piers which was usual until the 14th century, when Peter became predominant. It was unfashionable after the Reformation because of its association with the Papacy, and was later thought of as a rustic name. It did not return to fashion until 1904, when James Barrie's *Peter Pan* was published, but it is now one of the most popular boys' names. A short form is Pete.

PETRONELLA, PETRONILLA *f.*
(petrōnel'e, petrōnil'e)

These are feminine diminutives of Petronius, the Roman family name which may originally have come from *petra*, meaning 'stone'. Petronilla was thought, erroneously, to have been the name of St. Peter's daughter, and because of this the name was popular in the Middle Ages. It was used as the feminine equivalent of Peter.

PETULA *f.* *(petu'le)*

from the Latin meaning 'seeker'. It is uncommon in Britain, but the singer Petula Clark has made the name better known.

PHILIP *m.* *(fil'ip)*

from the Greek meaning 'lover of horses'. It was common in the Middle

Ages, on account of the Apostle of that name. In Elizabeth I's reign Philip of Spain was the arch enemy of England, and the name suffered accordingly. It was revived in the 19th century and is now common, the best known bearer at present being Prince Philip, Duke of Edinburgh. Phil is now the most usual short form, although the older Pip is sometimes used.

PHILIPPA *f.* (*fil'ipē*)

This is the feminine form of Philip (q.v.), but originally only used to distinguish women named Philip, in Latin records. Its use as a separate name dates from about the 19th century. It is now quite popular and is often abbreviated to Pippa, an Italian form.

PHOEBE *f.* (*fē'bi*)

from the Greek meaning 'the shining one'. It is one of the titles given by the Greeks to their moon-goddess. It occurs in St. Paul's Epistle to the Romans and, perhaps for this reason, was adopted after the Reformation, reaching its peak of popularity in the 17th century. It is still found, but is not popular,

PHYLLIS, PHILLIS f. (fil'is)

from the Greek meaning 'leafy'. In Greek legend it was the name of a girl who died for love and was transformed into an almond tree. It was used as a name for country girls in pastoral poetry and so became unfashionable until its 19th century revival. It is now very popular. Phyllida is an alternative form which is sometimes found.

POLLY *see* PAULINE, MARY

PRIMROSE f. (prim'rōs)

This flower name was popular at the beginning of the 20th century. Earlier examples in the 18th century probably derived from the Scottish surname.

PRISCILLA f. (prisil'e)

This is the Latin diminutive of *prisca*, meaning 'ancient'. It was the name of a woman mentioned in the Acts of the

Apostles. She was the wife of the Roman Jew Aquila, (Acts XVIII.2.). As with other New Testament names it was a favourite with the 17th century Puritans. It also appears as Prisca but this form is obsolete. Priscilla is now rather rare.

PRUDENCE *f.* (*prōo′dẹns*)

Prudence first appears in Chaucer, and it was one of the first abstract virtues to be adopted as a name by the Puritans. It is one of the few to have survived in use to the present day, and is now usually abbreviated to Prue.

PRUNELLA *f.* (*prōonel′ẹ*)

from the French meaning 'prune-coloured'. Its history is obscure, and it has never been in common use in Britain.

Q

QUEENIE *f.* (*kwē′ni*)

This name is sometimes given independently, but it is really a pet name for

Regina, which is Latin for 'queen'. The latter was used from the Middle Ages, possibly with reference to the Virgin Mary, Queen of Heaven. Queenie was also used as a nickname for girls christened Victoria during Queen Victoria's long reign. Not popular today.

QUENTIN, QUINTIN m. (*kwen'tin, kwin'tin*)

from the Roman clan Quintian, whose simple way of life made them famous among the lavish Romans. Quentin was the French form which the Normans introduced to England. It became obsolete after the Middle Ages except in Scotland. Its revival in the 19th century was probably due to Sir Walter Scott's historical romance *Quentin Durward*. It may also have been used occasionally as a given name for a fifth child.

R

RAB, RABBIE *see* **ROBERT**

RACHEL *f. (rā′chel)*

from the Hebrew for 'ewe', which was symbolic of gentleness and innocence. In the Book of Genesis Rachel was the daughter of Laban who was 'beautiful and well-favoured', and for whose hand Jacob served seven years (Gen. XXIX.20). In Britain the name was adopted after the Reformation, and it was very popular in the 17th and 19th centuries. The usual pet forms today are Rach, Rachie, Rae and Ray.

RACHIE *see* **RACHEL**

RADULF *see* **RALPH, RAOUL**

RAE, RAY *see* **RACHEL, RAYMOND**

RAFF, RAUF, *see* **RALPH**

RAFFAELO *see* **RAPHAEL**

RALF *see* **RALPH**

RALPH *m. (ralf′, rāf)*

from the Old Norse meaning 'counsel wolf'. In the earlier form, Radulf, this name was fairly common in England before the Norman Conquest, and it was reinforced by the French use. The medieval spellings were Ralf, Rauf and Raff(e) which were pronounced *rāf*. Ralf occurs from the 16th century, Rafe was the common form in the 17th century and Ralph appears in the 18th century. These names were all pronounced *rāf* until quite recently, when there has been a return to the earlier *ralf* (*see* RAOUL, ROLF).

RANALD *see* RONALD

RANDAL(L) *see* RANDOLPH

RANDOLPH *m.* (*ran'dolf*)

from Old English Randwulf, meaning 'shield wolf'. In the Middle Ages the forms Ranulf and Randal were used. The latter was latinised as Randulfus, and it was from this form that Randolph was coined in the 18th century. Randall and Randolph are sometimes used today. A well-known example is Randolph Churchill, son of Sir Winston Churchill.

RANDULPHUS *see* RANDOLPH

RANULF *see* **RANDOLPH**

RAOUL *m.* (*rowl', ra'ôôl*)

This is the French equivalent of Ralph
(q.v.), derived from Radulf. It was used
in Britain after the Norman Conquest,
but died out with the decline of French
speaking in this country. It has been
used occasionally in the 20th century,
possibly because of the large number of
soldiers who fought in France in two
World Wars.

RAPHAEL *m.* (*raf'āẹl*)

from the Hebrew meaning 'God has
healed'. In the Book of Tobit, in the
Apocrypha, it was the name of the archangel who helped Tobias. In England
the name has been used almost exclusively by Jews, although it is more general
in Italy. The most famous holder of the
name was Raffaelo Sanzio, who is
known by the name Raphael, and was
one of the great painters of the Italian
Renaissance.

RAY *see* **RAYMOND**

RAYMOND *m.* (rā′mɘnd)

from the Old German meaning 'counsel protection'. The Normans brought the name to Britain and it was particularly popular in crusading times. Two 13th century saints bore the name. One of them spent much of his life rescuing Spaniards captured by the Moors. Today the name is more popular than ever before. Its abbreviation Ray is sometimes given independently. There is a feminine Raymonde, which also has the short forms Ray and Rae.

REBECCA *f.* (rɘbek′ɘ)

In Hebrew this means a 'noose' or 'knotted cord' and, since this has the quality of not being able to slip, it came to mean a 'faithful wife'. In the Old Testament Rebekah was the wife of Isaac, and was renowned for her beauty. It was a favourite name among the Puritans, who took it to North America. Daphne du Maurier's classic novel

Rebecca, which was an equally popular film, may have done something towards reviving the name, although it is still uncommon. Becky is the short form.

REBEKAH *see* REBECCA

REDMOND *m.* (*red'mend*)

from the Old English meaning 'counsel protector'. It is rarely found in Britain.

REG, REGGIE *see* REGINALD

REGENWEALD *see* REYNOLD

REGINA *see* QUEENIE

REGINALD *m.* (*rej'ineld*)

This name has the same origin as Reynold (q.v.) and appears first as Reginaldus, a latinised form of this name. Reginald appears in the 15th century and seems to have started as a more formal alternative to Reynold. Neither name was common between the 15th and 19th centuries, but Reginald was then revived and became very common. It can be abbreviated to Reg, Reggie or Rex (*see* RONALD).

REGINALDUS *see* REGINALD

REINALD *see* REYNOLD

RENÉ(E) *m. and f.* (ré'nā)

These are French names derived from Latin *renatus*, meaning 'reborn'. The Latin form was sometimes used by Puritans in the 17th century, and the French forms have been used in Britain in the 20th century.

RENIE *see* IRENE

REUBEN *m.* (rōō'ben)

from the Hebrew meaning 'behold a son'. In Biblical times it was sometimes given to the son born to replace a child who had died, and it appears in the Bible as the name of a son of Jacob. Today it is used mostly by Jewish families (*see* RUFUS).

REX *m.* (reks)

This is the Latin for 'king' which has only been used as a Christian name in recent times. It is also found as an abbreviation of Reginald and Eric (qq.v.).

REYNARD *m.* (re′nàd)

from the Old German meaning 'mighty and brave'. This and Rainard were the Norman French forms, but they never became as common as Reynold, with which they were often confused. It is very rare today.

REYNAUD *see* REYNOLD

REYNOLD *m.* (ren′eld)

from Old English Regenweald, meaning 'power force'. This was not a common Anglo-Saxon name but it was reinforced at the time of the Norman Conquest by the French equivalent Reinald, or Reynaud. It was quite common up to the 15th century, by which time Reginald (q.v.) was superseding it (*see* RONALD).

RHODA *f.* (rō′de)

Derived from the Greek for 'rose', this is a New Testament name (Acts

X.11-13.), that was taken into use in the 17th century. It is still used occasionally.

RHODRI see RODERICK

RHONA, RONA see ROWENA

RHONWEN see ROWENA

RHYS m. (*rēs'*)

a common Welsh name meaning 'rashness'. The popularity of this name is due to the ancient Welsh family of this name. A Prince Rhys checked the Norman advance into Wales, and his grandson was appointed by Henry II as his Welsh deputy. It was a man called Rhys ap Thomas who had the power in Wales to establish Henry VII's dominion over it.

RICARD see RICHARD

RICEHARD see RICHARD

RICHARD m. (*rich'ĕd*)

This name first appears in Anglo-Saxon as Ricehard, meaning 'a hard ruler', which was later developed into Ricard. It was the Normans who spread the present form of the name, the softer, French, Richard. Richard Coeur-de-Lion's fame as a crusader gave the name great popularity, which was only slightly subdued by the bad reputations of the second and third English kings of this name. The short form Dick(e) appears as early as the 13th century, and this is still very common, though Rich(ie), Dickie, Rick(ie), Dickon and many others, have been used at various times. Richard is one of the commonest boys' names in Britain today.

RICK, RICKIE *see* **RICHARD, DEREK, ERIC**

RITA *f.* (rē′tę)

an abbreviation of Margarita (*see* MARGARET). It is also used as a separate name, and may have been popularised in the 20th century by the film star Rita Hayworth.

ROB, ROBIN *see* **ROBERT**

ROBERT *m.* (*rob'ęt*)

This name is derived from the Old German meaning 'fame bright'. Although there was an equivalent Anglo-Saxon name, it was the French form which took hold in Britain after the Norman Conquest. Robert Bruce popularised the name in Scotland where it has the local short forms Rab and Rabbie. Bob, Bobbie and Bert are used in England. Robin was a French diminutive of Rob, which came to Britain in the Middle Ages, and is now equally popular as a name in its own right.

ROBERTA, ROBINA *f.* (*rębęrt'e, rębĕn'e*)

These are feminine forms of Robert (q.v.) and Robin. Both have been used mainly in Scotland though there are exceptions. Oliver Cromwell's sister was called Robina. They were probably most common in the 19th century, and are seldom used today.

ROBIN *see* ROBERT

RODERICK m. (*rod'erik*)

from the Old German meaning 'fame rule'. The Goths took the name to Spain where it became Rodrigo, and it was established there at least as early as the 8th century. In Britain the name is most common in Scotland where it was originally used to transliterate a Gaelic name meaning 'red'. In Wales it is used as a modern equivalent of the Welsh Rhodri, meaning 'crown ruler'.

RODGE *see* **ROGER**

RODNEY m. (*rod'ni*)

This means 'reed island', and was originally a surname taken from the name of the Somerset village Rodney Stoke. It was not used as a Christian name until Admiral George Rodney gave it heroic associations in the 18th century. Since then it has become widespread.

RODRIGO *see* **RODERICK**

ROGER m. (roj'ę)

Hrothgar, meaning 'fame spear', was
an Anglo-Saxon name, but is was the
Normans who gave us the present form,
which was derived from an Old German
equivalent. Roger was a favourite
name in the Middle Ages. From the
16th-19th centuries it was mainly a
peasant name, but today it is widespread and more common than ever.
The ancient short form Hodge, once a
type-name for a farm labourer, has been
replaced by Rodge.

ROLAND m. (rō'lęnd)

from Old German Hrodland, meaning
'fame land'. Roland was the most
famous of Charlemagne's peers, and it
was the Normans who brought the
name to England in this form. The
ballad of *Childe Rowland*, an old story
about a son of King Arthur, shows the
usual spelling of the name up to the
19th century. It was very common in
the Middle Ages owing to its literary
associations, particularly the *Chanson*

de Roland, a 12th century French epic. Orlando is the Italian version which was popular in the 15th and 16th centuries. Roland is still very popular.

ROLF *m. (rolf)*

from Old German meaning 'fame wolf'. This name developed in Normandy and came to Britain at the time of the Norman Conquest. It was quite soon absorbed into Ralph (q.v.) but was revived in the late 19th century and is still current. Rollo is a latinisation. Rollo the Ganger ('Walker') was a 9th century Norwegian exile who, with his followers, founded the Norman race.

ROLLO *see* ROLF

RONALD *m. (ron'eld)*

Ronald and Ranald are Scottish equivalents of Reynold and Reginald (q.v.), but they are of Norse not Old English derivation. Ranald is still exclusively Scottish but Ronald is now widespread.

Diminutive forms commonly used are Ron and Ronnie.

RORY, RORIE *m.* (*raw′ri*)

from the Celtic meaning 'red'. The name became popular in Ireland due to the fame of the 12th century King Rory O'Connor. It is also widely used in the Highlands, and is sometimes used in England as an abbreviation of Roderick (q.v.).

ROSA *see* ROSE

ROSABEL, ROSABELLA, ROSALBA *see* ROSE

ROSALIA *see* ROSALIE

ROSALIE *f.* (*roz′ẹli, rōz′ẹli*)

probably from Latin *rosalia*. This is the name of a Roman festival, when garlands of roses were draped on tombs. Its use as a Christian name is due to St. Rosalia, a 12th century hermit, and the patron saint of Palermo. Rosalie is the French form which is sometimes borrowed in this country.

ROSALIND *f.* (*roz'ęlind*)

The origin of this name is the Old German Roslindis, meaning 'horse serpent'. When the Goths took it to Spain it was interpreted as *rosa* and *linda*, 'pretty rose', and it was with this meaning that it came over to Britain in Elizabeth I's reign. It was used by Shakespeare for the heroine of *As You Like It* and in another form, Rosaline, in two other plays. Largely due to this romantic literary association, it has been popular ever since.

ROSALINE *see* **ROSALIND**

ROSAMUND, ROSAMOND *f.*
(*roz'ęmęnd*)

from the Old German meaning 'horse protection'. It has generally been associated with the Latin *rosa munda*, meaning 'pure rose'. The Normans brought the name to England and, unlike most names of Germanic origin, it survived the Renaissance. It was usually spelt Rosamond in the French fashion, but both forms are used today.

ROSE *f.* (*rōz*)

This is the most popular of all flower
names which are used as personal names,
but it has an older and quite different
derivation. Its source is the Old German
hros, meaning 'horse'. (*see* ROSALIND,
ROSAMUND). The name was brought to
England by the Normans, and it has
been consistently popular, giving rise
to many derivatives, like Rosalba 'white
rose', Rosetta 'little rose' and Rosabel(la)
'beautiful rose'. Rosa is a Latin form
which has been used occasionally since
the 19th century.

ROSEMARY *f.* (*rōz'mẹri*)

This is generally considered to be a
borrowed plant name, although it is
sometimes thought of as a combination
of Rose and Mary. The plant name is
derived from the Latin *ros* and *marinus*
meaning 'dew' and 'of the sea'. It was
probably first used in 1745 and was for a
long time confined to one family. But

in the 20th century it has become wide-spread and very popular.

ROSLINDIS *see* ROSALIND

ROSS *m.* (*ros*)

from the Gaelic meaning 'of the peninsula', the name of a famous Scottish clan. It is popular in Scotland.

ROWENA *f.* (*rōē'nę*)

from the Welsh Rhonwen, meaning 'slender fair' or 'fair lance'. There was a Rowena in the 5th century, the daughter of the Jutish ruler Hengist, who fell in love with Vortigern, a Celtic chieftain. Its modern use is due to Sir Walter Scott, who gave the name to the heroine of his novel *Ivanhoe* in the 19th century. Variant forms are Rowina and Rhona.

ROXANA, ROXANE *f.* (*roks'ànę, roksan'*)

These are anglicised forms of Persian Raokshna which means 'brilliant one'. Roxana was the name of Alexander the Great's wife.

ROY m. (roi)

from the Celtic meaning 'red'. This name is often mistakenly thought to derive from the French word for 'king'. A well-known example of the name is the famous Highlander, Robert Macgregor, commonly known as Rob Roy because of his red hair, and who was involved in the Rising of 1715. In the 20th century it is well known in all English speaking countries. Sir Walter Scott's novel *Rob Roy*, may have contributed to its popularity.

RUBY f. (rōō'bi)

This is one of many jewel names that were taken into use during the 19th century.

RUDOLF, RUDOLPH m. (rōō'dolf)

from Old German Hrodulf, meaning 'fame wolf', Rudolf is the Modern German form of the name which has only been used in this country for about a hundred years. Earlier examples occurred only among German immigrants. The spread of this name was undoubtedly helped by the widespread adoration of Rudolf Valentino, the American film star, and also by *The Prisoner of Zenda*, Anthony Hope's novel, in which the hero is an Englishman called Rudolph Rassendyl.

RUDYARD *m.* (*rud'īàd*)

from an Old English place name, possibly meaning 'red enclosure'. This name is best known for Rudyard Kipling (1865-1936) the great writer on India. Kipling was christened Rudyard after the Lake in Staffordshire, where his parents had first met.

RUFUS *m.* (*rōō'fẹs*)

This is a Latin word meaning 'red-haired'. William Rufus was the second son of William the Conqueror, and king William II of England. The name has been used by Jews as an equivalent of Reuben (q.v.).

RUPERT m. (róo'pet)

This name has the same origin as Robert (q.v.) and means 'bright fame'. It developed in Germany, where it became Rupprecht, and Rupert is an English transliteration. Rupert of the Rhine was Charles I's nephew and a brilliant General and a scientist. He came to England to support the Royalist cause and was much admired for his dashing bravery. It was because of him that the English form was coined and became popular. An equally romantic figure in modern times was the poet Rupert Brooke, who died in the First World War aged 27. He may have helped to keep the name in common use.

RUPPRECHT see **RUPERT**

RUSSELL m. (rus'el)

This is primarily a surname and is derived from the French *rousseile*, which means 'little red one'. It came into use as a Christian name along with other family famous names in the 19th century. Rus(s) and Rusty are pet forms.

RUTH *f.* (*rŏŏth*)

from Hebrew, possibly meaning 'vision of beauty'. It was a common name just after the Reformation on account of the Old Testament heroine who gave her name to the *Book of Ruth*. The qualities attached to Ruth in the Bible are faithfulness and devotion. The name was also associated with the abstract noun, ruth, meaning 'sorrow' or 'pity'. It is still used fairly frequently.

S

SABIN(A) *m. and f.* (*sab'in, sabēn'e̥*)

Sabinus and Sabina are Latin names meaning respectively a Sabine man and woman. These have survived in England as Sabin and Sabina on account of two early saints who bore the name. Only the feminine form has survived as a Christian name; it is very rarely used.

SABINUS *see* **SABIN**

SABRINA *f. (sebrēn'e̯)*

from the Latin meaning 'from the boundary line', and the Latin name of the river Severn. Milton used it for the spirit of the river in his play *Comus*. In the 20th century, the play *Sabrina Fair* by Samuel Taylor, and the film into which it was made, caused the name to be better known.

SACHEVERELL *m. (seshev'erel)*

This is an old family name. It has been suggested that it originated as a Norman nickname, Sans Cheverel, meaning 'without leather'. Its use as a Christian name dated from the early 18th century when a Dr. Sacheverell was a Tory preacher. The best known example in this century is Sacheverell Sitwell the writer, but the name is not now in general use.

SADIE *see* **SARAH**

SAIREY, SAREY *see* **SARAH**

SAL, SALLY see SARAH

SALAMON see SOLOMON

SALLY f. (sal'i)

originally a pet name for Sarah (q.v.), but nowadays used separately.

SALOME f. (selōm'i, sa'lōmā)

This is the Greek form of an Aramaic name meaning 'peace of Zion'. In the New Testament it is the name of one of the women who looked after Jesus, and was the first person at his tomb on Easter Sunday. This led to its use in Britain in the 17th century among Puritans. However, the most famous holder of the name was another New Testament character, Salome, daughter of Herodias, who is infamous for causing the beheading of John the Baptist. Oscar Wilde wrote a play, *Salomé*, about this woman, and the name is primarily associated with her story. This may be partly responsible for its unpopularity today.

SAM *see* **SAMUEL**

SAMANTHA *f.* (s*e*man'th*e*)

from Aramaic meaning 'a listener'. This is a rare name in Britain but gradually becoming more widely known.

SAM(P)SON *m.* (sam's*e*n)

from the Hebrew meaning 'child of the sun'. In the Book of Judges, in the Old Testament, Samson was a judge, and champion of the Israelites against the Philistines. He was famous for his great strength. The Normans brought the name to England, and the French spelling Sanson was also used. The name continued in use until the 17th century, when it had a brief increase in popularity as a Biblical name, but faded out soon after the restoration of the monarchy.

SAMUEL *m.* (sam'ū*e*l)

from the Hebrew meaning 'heard by God', or 'asked of God'. The two Books of Samuel in the Old Testament tell how the prophet was the leader of the Israelites until they demanded a king, how he had to anoint Saul, and later trained David to replace him. This name was rare in Britain until after the Reformation, when it became a favourite. It is less common today and is usually shortened to Sam. In Scotland and Ireland it was for a long time used to transliterate the Gaelic Somhairle, a name derived from Old Norse and meaning 'summer wanderer', or 'Viking.'

SANCHIA *see* CYNTHIA

SANCHIA *f.* (*san'chie*)

This is a Provençal and Spanish name derived from Latin *sanctus*, meaning 'holy'. The name came to England in the 13th century when the Earl of Cornwall married Sanchia, daughter of the Count of Provence. The name then took many forms including Sence, Science and Saint. The original form survived and is still used occasionally.

SANDRA *f.* (sàn'drẹ, san'drẹ)

This is a short form of Italian Alessandra, now used as a name in its own right (*see* ALEXANDRA).

SANDY *see* **ALEXANDER**

SANSON *see* **SAMSON**

SARA(H) *f.* (se'rẹ)

from the Hebrew meaning 'princess', and the name of Abraham's wife in the Old Testament. This name was not common until the Reformation but it was very popular in the 17th and 18th centuries. During this period it was familiarly rendered Sa(i)rey e.g. Dickens' character in *Martin Chuzzlewit*, Sairey Gamp, who always carried a bulky umbrella. Sal(ly) and Sadie are pet forms. In Ireland Sarah has been used to render the Irish Sorcha, meaning 'bright', and Saraid, meaning 'excellent'. Sarah is a fairly common girl's name in Britain today.

SARAID *see* **SARAH**

SAUL m. (sawl)

from the Hebrew meaning 'asked for'. This name occurs in the Old Testament as the name of the first King of Israel, and in the New Testament as St. Paul's name before his conversion. It was first used as a Christian name in Britain in the 17th century, and has been used occasionally since.

SEAN m. (shawn')

This is the Irish form of John (q.v.) and developed from the French Jean. The variant form Shane, which is pronounced the same way, was an early phonetic rendering of the name in English, though in North America it has now come to be pronounced *shān*, as in the famous cowboy film of that name.

SEB, SEBBIE *see* SEBASTIAN

SEBASTIAN m. (sebast'ien)

from Latin Sebastianus, meaning 'man of Sebastia'. The name of this town in Asia Minor was derived from the Greek meaning 'majestic' or 'venerable'. St. Sebastian was executed by being shot at with arrows, and his martyrdom was a particularly popular subject of medieval painting. The name took hold in Spain, and in France, where it was shortened to Bastien, and taken across the Channel from Brittany to the West Country by fishermen. The form Bastian took root there. The name did not spread to the rest of Britain until modern times, but Sebastian is now reasonably common, having the short forms Seb and Sebbie.

SEBASTIANUS *see* **SEBASTIAN**

SECUNDA *see* **SECUNDUS**

SECUNDUS *m.* (*sekūn'des*)

This is the Latin word for 'second' and was sometimes used in Victorian times as a Christian name for a second child or son. Secunda was the feminine form.

SELENE *see* **SELINA**

SELEWINE *see* **SELWYN**

SELINA *f.* (sĕlē'nŏ)

The etymology of this name is disputed. One possible derivation is from Selene, the Greek for 'moon'; another from the Latin name Coelina, from *caelum*, meaning 'heaven', through the French form Céline *sălen'*. Celina is found in the Middle Ages which rather confirms the second theory. The name has never been common.

SELWYN *m.* (sel'win)

from Old English *selewine*, meaning 'house friend'. The surname Selwyn occurs in the 13th century but its use as a Christian name seems to date only from the 19th century, when it became common for distinguished surnames to be used as Christian names by the general public. The best known example is the Conservative politician, Selwyn Lloyd.

SEPTIMUS *m.* (sep'timŏs)

This is the Latin word for 'seventh'. It was used as a Christian name in the

19th century when large families were common, though it was occasionally used out of its numerical context. Septima was the feminine form.

SERAFINA *see* **SERAPHINA**

SERAPHINA *f.* (*serə̱fē'nə̱*)

This is a Latin derivative of the Hebrew meaning 'burning' or 'passionate one'. St. Seraphina was an Italian abbess of the 15th century. The name has been used, though very rarely, since the 19th century, and is sometimes spelt Serafina.

SERENA *f.* (*sə̱'rānə̱, sə̱'rēnə̱*)

This is the feminine form of Latin *serenus*, meaning 'calm', 'serene'. It has been used occasionally in modern times.

SEUMAS *see* **HAMISH, JAMES**

SEXTUS *m.* (*seks'tə̱s*)

This is the Latin for 'sixth', and was sometimes used in the 19th century for either a sixth son or a sixth male child.

SHAMUS *m.* (shā′mus)

This is a modern phonetic version of Seumus, which is the Irish for James (q.v.).

SHANE *see* **SEAN**

SHEILA *f.* (shē′lẹ)

This is a phonetic spelling of the Irish name Sile, which was derived from Celia (*see* CECILIA). Sheila is now a popular name throughout Britain.

SHE(E)NA *f.* (shē′nẹ)

This is a phonetic form of Sine which is the Irish for Jane (q.v.).

SHEPHERD *m.* (shep′ẹd)

The word 'shepherd' is derived from Old English, and is found both as a surname and Christian name today.

SHERLOCK *m.* (shẹr′lok)

from the Old English meaning 'fair-haired'. This name was immortalised by Sir Arthur Conan Doyle in his detective stories about Sherlock Holmes.

SHIMEON *see* **SIMEON, SIMON**

SHIRLEY *f.* (*she'li*)

This was originally a place name meaning 'shire meadow', and from this it became a surname in Yorkshire and elsewhere. Charlotte Brontë started the fashion for it as a girls' Christian name in 1849, when her novel of that name appeared. The name became popular in the U.S.A., where the child film star Shirley Temple was born. It was chiefly the admirers of this child star who made the name popular in Britain.

SHUSHANAH *see* **SUSAN**

SIBYL, SYBIL *f.* (*sib'el*)

In classical times the Sibyls were prophetesses, and some of them were supposed to have foretold the coming of Christ. Because of this, Sibylla came to be used as a Christian name, the Normans bringing it with them to England, where it became common in several forms. Sybil had a revival in the second half of the 19th century after Disraeli had published his political novel of that name (1845). Dame Sybil Thorndike the actress is a famous example in Britain.

SIBYLLA *see* SIBYL

SID *see* SIDNEY

SIDNEY, SYDNEY *m.* (*sid'ni*)

This is a surname which has its origin in the French place name St. Denis. The Sidney family came to England from France in Henry II's reign. Two great historical characters caused the name to be taken into use as a Christian name. The first was the Elizabethan soldier and poet, Sir Philip Sidney. The second was Algernon Sidney the 17th century republican, later idolised by the Whig party. The spelling Sydney, did not appear until the 19th century, and the city in Australia was named after Viscount Sydney, who was Secretary of State at the time. Nowadays the short form Sid is better known.

SIEGFRIED *m.* (*sēg′frēd*)

from the Old German meaning 'victory peace'. This name was first used in Britain at the end of the 19th century, due largely to the cult for Wagner's music, which was greatest at that time. Siegfried is the name of the mythical hero of Wagner's opera cycle *The Ring*. Siegfried Sassoon is a famous British poet.

SILAS *m.* (*sī′lĕs*)

This is a shortening of Silvanus, the name of the Roman god of trees. Silas appears in the Acts of the Apostles as the name of a colleague of St. Paul, though he is called Silvanus in the epistles. Both forms were used after the Reformation but only Silas became at all common, and neither is much in use today.

SILE *see* **SHEILA**

SILVANUS *see* **SILAS**

SILVESTER, SYLVESTER m.
(silvest'e)

Silvester is Latin for a 'wood-dweller'. There have been three popes of this name; the first one baptised the Roman Emperor Constantine and is said to have cured him of leprosy, and another in the 10th century invented the pendulum clock. The name was quite common in both forms in the Middle Ages and it has survived to the present day. Sylvester is now the more popular of the two.

SILVIA, SYLVIA f. (sil'vie)

This is the feminine form of Latin Silvius, meaning 'of the wood'. Rhea Silvia was the mother of Romulus and Remus, the founders of Rome. This may have been the reason why the name was adopted during the Renaissance in Italy. Like other classical names, it came to England in Elizabethan times. Shakespeare used it in *Two Gentlemen of Verona*, and this probably gave rise to its widespread use in Britain. The diminutive form is Sylvie.

SIMEON m. *(sim'iẹn)*

from Hebrew Shimeon, meaning 'listening'. This has the same origin as Simon (q.v.). The translators of the Bible into English used this form in the Old Testament. In the New Testament it is the name of the old man who blessed the baby Jesus in the Temple, and first recited the Nunc Dimittis. Simeon was used in Britain in the Middle Ages and again after the Reformation, but is uncommon now.

SIMON m. *(sī'mẹn)*

This is the better known English form of Shimeon, from the Hebrew meaning 'listening' (*see* SIMEON). The popularity of Simon in the Middle Ages was due to Simon Peter, the Apostle, whose popularity was great at that period. Like Peter, it went out of fashion after the Reformation because of its Roman Catholic associations, and it has never had the same popularity since, though it is now becoming fashionable again.

SINCLAIR m. (sin'cler)

This is a contraction of St. Clair, a town in Normandy (c.f. Sidney). The Normans brought the name to England and it developed as a surname, mainly in Scotland. It has been used as a Christian name at least since the 19th century.

SINE see JANE

SIS, SISLEY see CECILIA

SOLLY see SOLOMON

SOLOMON m. (sol'emen)

from Hebrew meaning 'little man of peace'. In the Old Testament King Solomon was renowned for his wisdom. The name was more often rendered Salamon in the Middle Ages. It died out, but was revived by Puritans after the Reformation. It is now used mostly by Jews. Solly is a frequently used abbreviation.

SOMERSET *m.* (*sum'eset*)

This is the name of the county, and is derived from the Old English meaning 'from the place of the summer settlers'. It was made famous as a Christian name by the 20th century writer Somerset Maugham.

SOMHAIRLE *see* SAMUEL

SONIA *f.* (*son'ie*)

This is a Russian diminutive form of Sophia (q.v.), and its use in Britain is recent, perhaps a result of the novel of this name by Stephen McKenna, published in 1917.

SOPHIA, SOPHIE *f.* (*sōfi'e, sō'fi*)

from the Greek meaning 'wisdom'. Sophia became a popular name in the Eastern Church on account of the great cathedral Hagia Sophia at Constantinople. The name spread through Hungary to Germany and hence to England, when George I became king. Both his mother and his wife bore this name.

Sophie is the anglicised form which was very popular in the 18th century. Its popularity waned at the end of the 19th century, but it is still in use.

SORCHA *see* **SARAH**

SPENCER *m.* *(spen'se)*

The earlier form of this name was Spenser, a surname which was a contraction of 'dispenser', an administrator of supplies in feudal times. The Le Despenser family came to power under Henry III, and by the 17th century the name had become Spencer, which was the form Sir Winston Churchill inherited. The name is also found in North America where it is rather more popular than in Britain.

SPENSER *see* **SPENCER**

STACEY *see* **ANASTASIA**

STAN *see* **STANLEY**

STANLEY *m.* *(stan'li)*

This was originally a surname derived from an old Anglo-Saxon place name meaning 'stony field', and hence probably meant a person from such a place. It was first used as a Christian name in the mid-19th century, because of its aristocratic connotation. The name later became popular, in imitation of the explorer John Rowlands, who adopted Stanley as a pseudonym. His fame led to the rapid spread of Stanley as a Christian name. It is still very common and has the short form Stan.

STEFFAN *see* STEPHEN

STELLA *f.* (stel'e)

This is the Latin word for 'star'. The earliest use of this name was by Roman Catholics. Stella Maris, meaning Star of the Sea, is used by them as a title of invocation of the Virgin Mary. The more general use of the name in modern times is due to its literary associations. An early literary use was in Sir Philip Sidney's *Astrophel and Stella*. In the early 18th century Swift used it as a pet name in various poems to Esther Johnson. Other forms are Estella and Estelle,

the former being used by Dickens in
the 19th century in his novel *Great
Expectations*.

STEPHANIE *f.* (*stef'eni*)

This is the French feminine form derived
from Latin Stephanus (*see* STEPHEN).
It is frequently used in Britain.

STEPHANUS *see* STEPHANIE

STEPHEN, STEVEN *m.* (*ste'ven*)

This name comes from the Greek
Stephanos meaning 'crown' or 'wreath'.
The laurel wreath was the highest honour
a man could attain in the classical
world. Stephen was a common personal
name in Ancient Greece, and it was borne
by the very first Christian martyr,
Stephen the Deacon (Acts VI & VII).
The name is first recorded in this country
in Domesday Book in the Latin from
Stephan(us). After the Norman Conquest
its popularity increased. Steve and Stevie
are the modern pet forms. There is also
a Welsh form Steffan.

STEVE, STEVIE *see* **STEPHEN**

STEWART *see* **STUART**

STUART *m.* (stū'ĕt)

from Old English *sti weard*, an official who looked after the animals kept for food. Though it has changed its meaning somewhat, it survives as 'steward' today. The man who founded the Royal House of Scotland was Walter the High Steward. Because of this, and the romantic associations of the name with the loyal cause of Scotland in the 18th century, Stuart and the alternative Stewart, are now common as surnames and as Christian names.

SUE, SUSIE, SUZY *see* **SUSAN**

SUSAN, SUSANNA(H) *f.* (sŏŏ'zĕn, sŏŏzan'ĕ)

Shushannah is Hebrew for 'lily' and Susanna(h) was the earliest form of this name in England, occuring in the Middle Ages, and becoming quite common after the Reformation. The Susanna mentioned in the New Testament (Luke VIII. 3) may have increased this popularity. Susan was adopted in the 18th century and superseded the earliest form completely in the 19th century. In the 20th century the French Suzanne and Suzette have also been used in Britain. Sue, Susie and Suzy are common short forms, and Susan is more popular today than ever before.

SUSANNA *see* **SUSAN**

SUZANNE, SUZETTE *see* **SUSAN**

SYBIL *see* **SIBYL**

SYDNEY *see* **SIDNEY**

SYLVESTER *see* **SILVESTER**

SYLVIA *see* **SILVIA**

T

TABITHA *f.* (*tab'ithę*)

from the Aramaic meaning 'gazelle'. In the New Testament (Acts IX) it is the name of a Christian woman of Joppa, who showed great charity towards the poor (*see* DORCAS). It was popular from the 17th to 19th centuries, but it is little used in Britain today.

TADHGH *see* TIMOTHY

TAFFY *see* DAVID

TALBOT *m.* (*tawl'bęt*)

Richard Talbot was a companion of William the Conqueror. It has been suggested that his name was probably a nickname, a combination of the French words *tailler*, meaning 'to cut' and *botte*, meaning 'faggot'. As a Christian name it was quite common in the 12th and 13th centuries. Nowadays it is more often found as a surname.

TALITHA *f.* (*talith'ę*)

from an Aramaic word meaning 'girl'. It has very occasionally been used in the 20th century.

TALMAI *see* BARTHOLEMEW

TAM, TAMMY *see* THOMAS

TAMASINE, TAMSIN
see **THOMASIN**

TANCRED *m. (tank′red)*

from the Old German meaning 'think counsel'. Tancred was the Norman form, which has occasionally been used in England since the Conquest.

TANYA *see* **TATIANA**

TATIANA *f. (tatiá′nę)*

This name has been popular in Russia for a long time, especially in its abbreviated forms Tanya and Tonya which are sometimes used in Britain. There were several saints named Tatianus, the masculine form, and a St. Tatiana, a martyr of the Greek Orthodox Church. Its derivation is obscure but probably Asiatic.

TATIANUS *see* **TATIANA**

TEBALD, TIBALD, TYBALT
see **THEOBALD**

TED, TEDDY *see* **EDMOND, EDWARD, THEODORE**

TEDDY *see* THEODORE

TERENCE *m.* (*ter'ens*)

from Latin Terentius, a Roman clan name of unknown meaning. It has only recently been used in this country having come from Ireland, where it is used to transliterate the native Turlough (q.v.). Terry is the short form.

TERESA, THERESA *f.* (*terä'ze, terē'se*)

It has been suggested that this name was originally spelt Therasia, which was the name of two Greek islands, and so meant a woman from that place. Otherwise its derivation is obscure. The first recorded Therasia was the wife of the 5th century St. Paulinus, and was responsible for his conversion. The name was for a long time confined to Spain, where it flourished until the 16th century. After this, St. Teresa of Avila spread the name to all Roman Catholic countries. But it did not become common in this country until the 18th century, when it was spread by the admirers of the Empress Maria Theresia of Austria. It is often abbreviated to Tess, Tessa or Tessie. The form Terry, shared with other masculine names, is also found. A variant is Trac(e)y.

TERRY *see* **TERENCE, TERESA**

TERRY *see* **THEODORIC**

TESS, TESSA, TESSIE *see* **TERESA**

TEWDWR *see* **THEODORE**

THELMA *f.* *(thel'mę, tel'mę)*

Like Mavis (q.v.) this name was invented in the 19th century by the novelist Marie Corelli, and spread quickly throughout the country. There is a Greek word *thelma*, meaning 'will', which may have had some influence on its development. It is generally pronounced *thel'mę*, and is now more common in North America than in Britain.

THEO *see* **THEOBALD, THEODORA, THEODORE**

THEOBALD m. (*thē'ębawld*)

from Old German Theudobald, meaning 'people bold'. Theobeald was the Anglo-Saxon form which was reinforced at the Conquest by the Norman Theobald. This settled down as Tebald, Tibald and Tybalt, but remained Theobaldus in Latin documents. The use of Tibs, Tibbles and Tibbie as a name for a cat comes from the medieval animal story *Reynard the Fox*, in which the cunning cat is called Tybalt. The abbreviation Theo is shared with other names having this stem.

THEOBALDUS *see* **THEOBALD**

THEODORA f. (*thēędaw'rę*)

This is the feminine form of Theodore (q.v.), which has been used occasionally since the 17th century. It is usually abbreviated to Theo.

THEODORE m. (*thē'ędaw*)

from the Greek meaning 'gift of God'. There are twenty eight saints of this name in the Church Calendar. One of them, a 7th century Archbishop of Canterbury, instituted the parish system. In England the name did not become general until the 19th century, but in Wales it has long had the form Tewdwr or Tudor, the name of the dynasty founded by Henry VII. The usual abbreviation in North America is Teddy, and the now universal teddy bear was thus named because of President Theodore Roosevelt's passion for big-game hunting. In England Theo is a more common abbreviation, though the name is now rare.

THEODORIC m. (thēod'erik)

from the Old German meaning 'people's ruler'. The Old English form of the name was Theodric which in medieval times became Terry, Theodoric became the most common form in the 18th century, but it is rare in Britain today.

THEODOSIA f. (thēodō'siẹ)

from the Greek meaning 'god-given'.

It has been used occasionally in Britain since the 17th century.

THEODRIC *see* THEODORIC

THEOPHANIA *f.* (*thē'ōfănie̯*)

from the Greek meaning 'the manifestation of God'. Tifaine was the Old French form, and this name was given to girls born at the time of Epiphany, the words having the same meaning. The name was introduced into England in the 13th century, and was the origin of several surnames, the best known of which is Tiffany. This has occasionally been used as a Christian name. All forms of the name are rare.

THEOPHILA *f.* (*thēof'ile̯*)

This is a rare feminine form of Theophilus (q.v.), it was occasionally used in the 17th century.

THEOPHILUS *m.* (*thēof'ile̯s*)

from the Greek meaning 'loved of God'. St. Luke addressed his Gospel and the Acts of the Apostles to a man of this name and, because of this, the name was fairly common in the 17th century among Puritans.

THERASIA, THERESIA *see* **TERESA**

THERESA *see* **TERESA**

THEUDOBALD *see* **THEOBALD**

THOMAS *m. (tom′əs)*

from the Aramaic meaning 'twin'. It was first given by Jesus to an Apostle named Judas, to distinguish him from Judas Iscariot and Jude. In England it occurs only as a priest's name until the Norman Conquest, after which it became common. The abbreviation Tom appears in the Middle Ages. The name was strengthened by the popularity of Thomas Becket, martyred in 1170, and from the 18th century it was one of the six most common men's names. Tam and Tammy are the Scottish pet forms. The nickname 'a Tommy' for a British private soldier goes back to the 19th century, when the enlistment form had on it the specimen signature 'Thomas

Atkins'. The tommy-gun was invented by a man called Thompson.

THOMASINA *see* THOMASIN

THOMASIN(E) *f.* (*tom'ǝsin*)

These are feminine diminutives of Thomas (q.v.). They have been used since the Middle Ages. Tamasine and Tamsin are West Country variants and there has been some revival of the latter in recent years. Thomasina is an old latinised version which was revived in the 19th century.

THOR *see* THURSTAN

THORA *f.* (*thaw'rǝ*)

from the Norse meaning 'dedicated to Thor'. Thor was the god of thunder in Norse mythology, and he also gave his name to 'Thursday'. Thora is a rare name in Britain.

THORKETILL *see* TORQUIL

THURSTAN *m.* (*thǝ'stǝn*)

from the Norse meaning 'Thor stone',

Thor was one of the principal Old Norse gods, and his name means 'thunder'. The Danes brought the name to England before the Norman Conquest and it has been in use ever since, though it is now rare.

TIBBIE, TIBBLES, TIBS
see **THEOBALD**

TIFAINE *see* **THEOPHANIA**

TIFFANY *see* **THEOPHANIA**

TILLY *see* **MATILDA**

TIM, TIMMY *see* **TIMOTHY**

TIMOTHEA *see* **TIMOTHY**

TIMOTHEOS *see* **TIMOTHY**

TIMOTHY m. (*tim'ẹthi*)

Timotheos is an old Greek name meaning 'honouring God'. Its use as a Christian name is due to Timothy, the companion of St. Paul. It was not used anywhere in Europe until the 16th century, when many classical and biblical names were revived. Tim and Timmy are the abbreviations. In Ireland Timothy has for a long time been used as an equivalent for the native Tadhgh which means 'poet'. It is one of the commonest boys' names in Britain today. Timothea is a rare feminine form.

TITUS *m.* (*tīt'es*)

This is a Latin name which, some suggest, is derived from a Greek root. Two well-known holders of the name were a follower of St. Paul, and, in contrast, the infamous Titus Oates, an English conspirator and perjurer of the 17th century. It is very rarely found today.

TOBIAS, TOBY *m.* (*tōbi'es, tō'bi*)

These are respectively the Greek and English forms of an Old Hebrew name which means 'the Lord is good'. The story of 'Tobias and the Angel', which is told in the Book of Tobit in the Apocrypha, was a favourite one in the Middle Ages. Punch's dog Toby is named after the dog that accompanied Tobias on his travels. The name was most common in the 17th century and the English form is still in use today. The 'Toby jug' is probably thus named in honour of a great 18th century drinker, Toby Philpot.

TOINETTE *see* **ANTONY**

TOM, TOMMY *see* **THOMAS**

TONI *see* **ANTONY**

TONY *see* **ANTONY**

TORCULL *see* **TORQUIL**

TORMOD *see* **NORMAN**

TORQUIL m. *(tawk'wil)*

This is the English rendering of the Norse name, Thorketill. The first element is the name of the Norse God Thor, and the rest is obscure of meaning. The original became Torcull in Gaelic, which was anglicised into Torquil. It is used in Scotland, especially among the Macleod family, and it has occasionally been given in England.

TOTTY *see* **CHARLOTTE**

TRAC(E)Y *see* **TERESA**

TREFOR *see* **TREVOR**

TREVOR *m.* (*trev'ę*)

from the Irish meaning 'wise'. Trefor is the Welsh version and Trevor is the English spelling of this.

TRICIA *see* **PATRICIA**

TRISTAN *see* **TRISTRAM**

TRISTRAM *m.* (*tris'trẹm*)

from Celtic Drystan, meaning 'tumult' or 'din'. Tristram occurs from the 12th century only, and it soon became confused with the French Tristan, derived from *triste*, meaning 'sad'. It is best known for *Tristram Shandy*, a famous 18th century novel by Laurence Sterne, and for the islands in the South Atlantic called Tristan da Cunha, after the Portuguese navigator who discovered them.

TRIXIE *see* **BEATRICE**

TRUDIE *see* **GERTRUDE**

TUDOR *see* **THEODORE**

TURLOUGH *see* **TERENCE**

TURLOUGH m. (*tẹ'lō*)

from the Irish meaning 'like Thor', the Norse god of thunder. The name took root in the days when Vikings settled in Ireland, where it is a common name, though nowadays often represented by Terence or Charles (qq.v.).

U

ULA f. (*ūl'ẹ*)

This is a rare name in Britain. It probably derives from the Old English word for 'owl'.

ULICK *see* **ULYSSES**

ULYSSES m. (*ū'lisēs*)

This is the Latin name for the Greek hero Odysseus, who conquered Troy, and whose tale is told in Homer's

Odyssey. Though little used in England, Scotland or Wales, it has often been used in Ireland as an equivalent for the Irish Ulick, meaning 'mind reward'. In 1922 James Joyce's famous novel *Ulysses* was published.

UMBERTO *see* HUMBERT

UNA *f.* (ŏŏ′nẹ, ū′nẹ)

The etymology of this ancient Irish name is obscure. The true Irish spelling of the name is Oonagh or Oona, both of which are also found in Scotland. Juno is another Irish form, best known for Sean O'Casey's play *Juno and the Paycock*. Una has been used in England, possibly on account of Rudyard Kipling's use of it for one of the two children in *Puck of Pook's Hill*.

UNITY *f.* (ū′niti)

This is one of the abstract virtue names that became quite common among Puritans after the Reformation. It is very rarely found today.

URSULA *f.* (*ĕs'ūlĕ*)

from the Latin meaning 'little she-bear'. The name was fairly common in, the Middle Ages on account of St. Ursula, a 5th century Cornish princess, who, with her companions, was killed by hostile inhabitants when shipwrecked near Cologne. The name had a revival in the mid 19th century when the novel, *John Halifax, Gentleman*, by Mrs Craik, became popular, in which the heroine's name was Ursula.

V

VAL *see* **VALERIE**

VALENTINE *m. and f.* (*val'ĕntīn*)

from Latin *valens*, meaning 'strong', or 'healthy'. St. Valentine was a 3rd century Roman priest whose martyrdom happened to fall on February 14th, the eve of the celebrations of the pagan goddess Juno, when lots were drawn to choose lovers. The pagan festival was absorbed by the Christian religion and is still celebrated today. The custom of sending cards was started in the 19th century. The name has been used in Britain since the 13th century and can be used for either sex. Valentina is an alternative feminine form. Val is a common diminutive, shared with Valerie.

VALERIE *f.* (*val'eri*)

Valérie was the French form of the Roman family name Valeria, and was taken into use in Britain in the late 19th century. It comes from the verb 'to be in good health' and is now quite common in Britain, having the short form Val.

VANESSA *f.* (*venes'e*)

This name was invented in the early 18th century by the poet Jonathan Swift as a pet name for Esther Vanhomrigh. He took the first syllable of her surname and added Essa, which was a pet form of Esther. The name is rather more common now than previously, the best known example being Vanessa Redgrave the actress.

VARIN see WARREN

VAUGHN, VAUGHAN m. (vawn)

from the Welsh Vychan, meaning 'small one'. It is not a common name, but a famous example is the composer Vaughan Williams.

VENETIA f. (venēsh'ie)

from the Celtic meaning 'blessed'. It is thought by some to represent the Latin form of the Welsh name Gwyneth (q.v.). It is unusual in Britain.

VERA f. (vēr'e)

This name has two possible derivations. One possible source is the Russian for 'faith', another is the Latin meaning 'true'. It was used in English literature in the 19th century, and became popular in Britain at the beginning of the 20th. It is sometimes used as an abbreviation of Veronica (q.v.).

VERILY *see* **VERITY**

VERITY *f.* (ver′iti)

from the English word for 'truth'. It was first used by the Puritans in the 17th century, and has been quite common ever since. The variant, Verily, is also found occasionally.

VERNA *f.* (ve′ne)

This is a Latin word meaning 'spring-like' and it is occasionally used as a Christian name in Britain today.

VERNON *m.* (ver′nen)

Richard de Vernon was one of the companions of William the Conqueror. The surname derives from a French place name which means 'little alder grove'. It was not used as a Christian name until the 19th century, when many such aristocratic names were taken into general use.

VERONICA *f.* (veron′ike)

from Latin *vera iconica*, meaning 'a

true image.' St. Veronica is the name given by tradition to the woman who wiped Christ's face when he was on his way to Calvary. A 'true image' of Christ's face was supposed to have appeared on the piece of rag she used. Véronique has long been popular in France, and it was from there that the name reached Scotland in the late 17th century. It does not appear much in England before the late 19th century, but is now fairly common. H. G. Wells' novel *Ann Veronica*, published in 1909, may have contributed to its popularity.

VÉRONIQUE *see* VERONICA

VIC *see* VICTOR

VICK, VICKIE, VICKY, VIKKI *see* VICTORIA

VICTOR *m.* (*vik'tẹ*)

This is Latin for 'conqueror'. Although it occurs in medieval England it was not common until the 19th century, when Victor was used as a masculine equivalent of Victoria (q.v.) and became very common. The common short form is Vic.

VICTORIA *f. (viktaw′rię)*

from the Latin meaning 'victory'. This name was hardly used in this country until the reign of Queen Victoria, who was named after her mother. The name has never been particularly fashionable, and today is more often found in one of its short forms, Vick(y), Vickie and Vikki. Vita and Viti and the pet name Queenie are also found.

VINCE *see* VINCENT

VINCENT *m. (vin′sęnt)*

from the Latin meaning 'conquering'. There was a 3rd century Spanish martyr of this name whose cult was widespread. The name occurs in English records from the 13th century and gave rise to the surnames Vincent, Vincey and Vince. It was, however, the 17th century St. Vincent de Paul who caused the name to be revived. He founded the Vincentian Order of the Sisters of

Charity. The name became quite common in the 19th century, and the usual short form is Vince.

VIOLA *f.* (*vī′olę*)

This is Latin for 'violet'. Although it does occur in the Middle Ages the modern use of this name is due to Shakespeare, who gave it to the heroine of *Twelfth Night*. It has never been as common as Violet (q.v.).

VIOLET *f.* (*vī′olęt*)

from Latin *viola*, through the Old French diminutive, Violete. This is one of the many flower names used as Christian names in this country. French influence took this name to Scotland in the 16th century and it became quite popular there. It did not spread to England until the 19th century. Violette and Violetta have also been used.

VIOLETTA, VIOLETTE *see* VIOLET

VIRGINIA *f.* (*vęjin′ię*)

Although there was a Roman family

called Virginus, the modern use of this name dates only from 1584, when Sir Walter Raleigh called his newly founded colony in North America, Virginia, after Elizabeth Tudor, the 'Virgin Queen'. It has always been popular in North America, but it did not become common in Britain until the mid 19th century. Ginny is a common pet form on both sides of the Atlantic.

VITA, VITI *see* VICTORIA

VITUS *see* GUY

VIV *see* VIVIAN, VIVIEN

VIVIAN *m.* (*viv'ien*)

from the Latin meaning 'lively'. This name occurs in the Latin form Vivianus from the late 12th century, but it has never become common. Sir Vivian Fuchs, the Antarctic explorer is probably the best-known contemporary example (*see* VIVIEN). A common short form is Viv.

VIVIANUS *see* **VIVIAN**

VIVIEN *f.* (*viv'i̯en*)

This is the feminine spelling of Vivian (q.v.) and comes from the French Vivienne. Tennyson gave the name some vogue in the 19th century when he wrote the poem based on Arthurian legend, called, *Vivien and Merlin*. Vivien Leigh the actress is a famous contemporary example, though the name is not common. The short form Viv is shared with Vivian.

VIVIENNE *see* **VIVIEN**

W

WAL, WALLY *see* **WALLACE, WALTER**

WALDHAR *see* **WALTER**

WALLACE *m.* (*wol'es*)

from the surname of Sir William Wallace, the great Scottish patriot of the 13th century. The use of his name as a Christian name started about a hundred years ago. The name is derived from the Old English meaning 'foreign'. Another spelling of the name is Wallis, and this form is popular in North America where it is used for both sexes. The short forms Wal and Wally are shared with Walter.

WALLIS *see* **WALLACE**

WALT, WAT *see* **WALTER**

WALTER m. (*wawl'tẹ*)

from Old German Waldhar, meaning 'rule people'. Walter was very popular among the Normans, and the name quickly became established in England, where, later on, it came to be pronounced *wawltẹ*. Sir Walter Raleigh is a well-known historical example; he used the short form Wat for his son. Walt, Wal and Wallis are more popular short forms today, and Walt is used as a separate name in North America. The 19th century novelist Sir Walter Scott may have contributed to the popularity of the name. Many surnames are derived from Walter and its short forms, including Watt(s), Watkin(s), Watson and Waters.

WALWAIN, WALWYN *see* GAWAIN

WANDA *f.* (won'dę)

This is a German feminine name of doubtful meaning. Its use in this country is recent, possibly starting when a novel of that name by Ouida was published in 1883.

WARNER *m.* (waw'nę)

from the Old German meaning 'Varin folk'. The Normans introduced the name to England as Garnier, which gave us the surnames Garner and Warner. It is largely through taking the surname as a Christian name that Warner has been used in modern times. It is particularly popular in North America.

WARREN *m.* (wor'ęn)

from the Old German folk-name Varin.

The Normans introduced the forms Warin and Guarin to England and these led to the surnames Warren, Waring and Garnet. It practically died out as a Christian name after the 14th century, though it remained in use where there were family connections with the surname. It became much more common in North America, and from there it is now filtering back into use in Britain.

WENDY *f.* (*wen'di*)

This name was first used by James Barrie in *Peter Pan* (1904). The name started as 'Friendy-Wendy' a pet name for Barrie used by a child friend of his, Margaret Henley. The name has become quite common since and is particularly popular in the acting profession.

WIDO *see* GUY

WILBUR *m.* (*wil'be*)

This name is very popular in North America but is practically unknown in

Britain. It has been suggested that it originated with Dutch settlers in America, and may come from Wildeboer, the Dutch for 'wild farmer'. Another possible source is the Old German Williburg, meaning 'resolute protection'. The most famous example was Wilbur Wright, who, with his brother Orville, made the first successful powered flight in 1903.

WILDEBOER *see* WILBUR

WILF *see* WILFRED

WILFRED, WILFRID m. (*wil'frid*)

from Old English Wilfrith, meaning 'will peace'. St. Wilfrid was an important figure in the 7th century, and his name was particularly popular in Yorkshire, where he preached and founded the sees of Ripon and Hexham. The name did not survive the Norman Conquest but was revived by the Tractarians in the 19th century. It is now fairly common, and has the pet form Wilf.

WILFRITH *see* WILFRED

WILHELMINA, WILMA *see* WILLIAM

WILL, WILLIE *see* WILLIAM

WILLA, *see* WILLIAM

WILLIAM *m. (wil'iem)*

from the Old German meaning 'will helmet'. William was always a popular name with the Normans, who brought it to England, and, until the 13th century when it was ousted by John, it was the commonest of all names in England. From the 16th-19th centuries William was about equal with John in popularity, and it has recently become very fashionable again. Numerous surnames are derived from it, including Williamson, Wilson, Wilcox, Wilmot, Wilkins, Wilkes, Willis etc. Will or Willie are the old short forms but Bill and Billie are more usual today. Feminine forms which have been used occasionally are Wilhelmina and Wilma, and short forms include Willa, Minnie and Minna. These feminine forms are more popular in America where the

German immigrants have spread their use.

WIN, WINNIE *see* WINIFRED

WINIFRED *f.* (*win'ifrid*)

from the Welsh feminine name Gwen-frewi, anglicised as Winifred and later confused with the Old English male name Winfrith, meaning 'friend of peace'. St. Winifred, a 7th century saint, was killed by Caradog, a chieftain from Hawarden in Flintshire. Although she was a popular saint in the Middle Ages, her name was not really used much until the 16th century. Win, Winnie and less often Freda, are short forms.

WINSTON *m.* (*win'stẹn*)

This is the name of a small village in Gloucestershire, and probably means 'friend's settlement'. The name has been used in the Churchill family since 1620, when Sir Winston Churchill, father of the 1st Duke of Marlborough, was born. His mother was Sarah

Winston. Despite the tremendous love and admiration which the British people had for the second Sir Winston Churchill, the name has not become common.

WYN, WYNNE *see* **GWYN**

WYNDHAM *m. (win'dem)*

from the Old English Windham, meaning 'from the enclosure with the winding path'. It is not a common name.

X

XANTHE *f. (zan'thi)*

from the Greek meaning 'yellow'. It has occasionally been used in Britain.

XENIA *f. (zen'ie)*

from the Greek meaning 'hospitable one'. It is only occasionally found.

Y

YEHUDI *see* **JUDE**

YOLANDE *f.* (*yoland'i*)

from the Greek meaning 'violet flower'. It has been used occasionally in Britain and North America.

YVES *see* IVOR, YVONNE

YVONNE, YVETTE *f.* (*ēvon', ēvet'*)

from the Old French meaning 'yew bow'. It is the feminine diminutive of the common Breton name Yves. The masculine name has never been common in Britain, but the feminine forms are quite popular.

Z

ZACCHAEUS *m.* (*zakē'ęs*)

This is a latinisation of Hebrew Zakkai, an abbreviation of Zachariah (*see* ZACHARIAS). In the New Testament (Luke XIX) Zacchaeus was the name of the publican who climbed into a tree to get a better view when Jesus passed by, and later entertained him at his house. The name was much used by Puritans in the 17th century but is now obsolete.

ZACHARIAH, ZACHARIAN
see **ZACHARIAS**

ZACHARIAS, ZACHARY *m.* (*zakĕrī'ĕs, zak'ĕri*)

These are respectively the Greek and English forms of the Hebrew Zachariah or Zechariah, meaning 'the Lord has remembered'. Zachary was used occasionally in the Middle Ages, but did not become at all common until the Puritans adopted it in the 17th century. They took it to America where it is still in use, together with the short form Zak.

ZAK *see* **ZACHARIAH**

ZAKKAI *see* **ZACCHAEUS**

ZENOBIA *f.* (*zenō'biĕ*)

This was the name of a great Queen of Palmyra in the 3rd century A.D. She ruled the Eastern Roman Empire, and her aggressive foreign policy made it necessary for Aurelian to wage war on her. This he did successfully, and put an end to her power, though he spared her life. The name occurs in Cornwall from the 16th century but the reason for this is unknown.

ZILLAH *f.* (*zil'ę*)

from the Hebrew for 'shade'. The name occurs in the Old Testament (Gen. IV, 19-23), and was used occasionally after the Reformation. Today it survives among gypsies.

ZOE *f.* (*zō'ē*)

This is the Greek word for 'life'. The Alexandrian Jews used it to translate the Hebrew equivalent for Eve into Greek, Eve being the 'mother of life'. The name spread throughout the Eastern Church but has only been used in Britain in the last hundred years. It is very rare still, though slightly more common in North America.